endorsed for BTEC

REVISE BTEC NATIONAL Business

REVISION WORKBOOK

Series Consultant: Harry Smith

Authors: Steve Jakubowski, Claire Parry, Jon Sutherland
and Diane Sutherland

While the publishers have made every attempt to ensure that advice on the qualification and its assessment is accurate, the official specification and associated assessment guidance materials are the only authoritative source of information and should always be referred to for definitive guidance.

This qualification is reviewed on a regular basis and may be updated in the future. Any such updates that affect the content of this Revision Workbook will be outlined at **www.pearsonfe.co.uk/BTECchanges**.

A note from the publisher

In order to ensure that this resource offers high-quality support for the associated Pearson qualification, it has been through a review process by the awarding body. This process confirms that this resource fully covers the teaching and learning content of the specification or part of a specification at which it is aimed. It also confirms that it demonstrates an appropriate balance between the development of subject skills, knowledge and understanding, in addition to preparation for assessment.

Endorsement does not cover any guidance on assessment activities or processes (e.g. practice questions or advice on how to answer assessment questions) included in the resource nor does it prescribe any particular approach to the teaching or delivery of a related course.

Pearson examiners have not contributed to any sections in this resource relevant to examination papers for which they had prior responsibility.

Examiners will not use endorsed resources as a source of material for any assessment set by Pearson.

Endorsement of a resource does not mean that the resource is required to achieve this Pearson qualification, nor does it mean that it is the only suitable material available to support the qualification, and any resource lists produced by the awarding body shall include this and other appropriate resources.

Pearson

Published by Pearson Education Limited, 80 Strand, London, WC2R 0RL.

www.pearsonschoolsandfecolleges.co.uk

Copies of official specifications for all Pearson qualifications may be found on the website: qualifications.pearson.com

Text and illustrations © Pearson Education Ltd 2017
Typeset and illustrated by Kamae Design, Oxford
Produced by Out of House Publishing
Cover illustration by Miriam Sturdee

The rights of Steve Jakubowski, Claire Parry, Jon Sutherland and Diane Sutherland to be identified as authors of this work have been asserted by them in accordance with the Copyright, Designs and Patents Act 1988.

First published 2017

20 19 18
10 9 8 7 6 5 4 3 2

British Library Cataloguing in Publication Data
A catalogue record for this book is available from the British Library

ISBN 978 1 2921 5011 6

Printed in Slovakia by Neografia

Acknowledgements

We are grateful to the following for permission to reproduce copyright material:

Tables

Tables on page 5, page 6 courtesy of Office for National Statistics licensed under the Open Government Licence v.3.0.; Table on page 13 used by permission of TVadvertising.co.uk

Text

Extract on page 4 adapted from http://www.ibisworld.co.uk/market-research/gyms-fitness-centres.html, used by permission of IBISWorld Ltd.; Article on page 4 adapted from The Leisure Database Company Ltd, used by permission; Articles on page 5, page 8 adapted from http://www.independent.co.uk/news/business/analysis-and-features/the-gym-group-proves-that-no-frills-pay-as-you-go-gyms-work-out-well-a6727996.html, used by permission of The Independent; Article on page 14 adapted from David Lloyd website, used by permission of David Lloyd Clubs.

Websites

Pearson Education Limited is not responsible for the content of any external internet sites. It is essential for tutors to preview each website before using it in class so as to ensure that the URL is still accurate, relevant and appropriate. We suggest that tutors bookmark useful websites and consider enabling students to access them through the school/college intranet.

Notes from the publisher

1 In order to ensure that this resource offers high-quality support for the associated Pearson qualification, it has been through a review process by the awarding body. This process confirms that this resource fully covers the teaching and learning content of the specification or part of a specification at which it is aimed. It also confirms that it demonstrates an appropriate balance between the development of subject skills, knowledge and understanding, in addition to preparation for assessment.

Endorsement does not cover any guidance on assessment activities or processes (e.g. practice questions or advice on how to answer assessment questions) included in the resource nor does it prescribe any particular approach to the teaching or delivery of a related course.

While the publishers have made every attempt to ensure that advice on the qualification and its assessment is accurate, the official specification and associated assessment guidance materials are the only authoritative source of information and should always be referred to for definitive guidance.

Pearson examiners have not contributed to any sections in this resource relevant to examination papers for which they have responsibility.

Examiners will not use endorsed resources as a source of material for any assessment set by Pearson.

Endorsement of a resource does not mean that the resource is required to achieve this Pearson qualification, nor does it mean that it is the only suitable material available to support the qualification, and any resource lists produced by the awarding body shall include this and other appropriate resources.

2 Pearson has robust editorial processes, including answer and fact checks, to ensure the accuracy of the content in this publication, and every effort is made to ensure this publication is free of errors. We are, however, only human, and occasionally errors do occur. Pearson is not liable for any misunderstandings that arise as a result of errors in this publication, but it is our priority to ensure that the content is accurate. If you spot an error, please do contact us at resourcescorrections@pearson.com so we can make sure it is corrected.

Introduction

This Workbook has been designed to help you revise the skills you may need for the externally assessed units of your course. Remember that you won't necessarily be studying all the units included here – it will depend on the qualification you are taking.

BTEC Level 3 National Qualification	Externally assessed units
Certificate	Unit 2 Developing a Marketing Campaign
Extended Certificate	Unit 2 Developing a Marketing Campaign Unit 3 Personal and Business Finance
Foundation Diploma	Unit 2 Developing a Marketing Campaign Unit 3 Personal and Business Finance
Diploma	Unit 2 Developing a Marketing Campaign Unit 3 Personal and Business Finance Unit 6 Principles of Management
Extended Diploma	Unit 2 Developing a Marketing Campaign Unit 3 Personal and Business Finance Unit 6 Principles of Management Unit 7 Business Decision Making

Your Workbook

Each unit in this Workbook contains either one or two sets of revision questions or revision tasks to help you **revise the skills** you may need in your assessment. The units use selected content and outcomes to provide an example of ways of applying your skills. The detail of the actual assessment may change so always make sure you are up to date. Ask your tutor or check the **Pearson website** for the most up-to-date **Sample Assessment Material** to get an indication of the structure of your assessment and what this requires of you.

Often, you will also find one or more useful features that explain or break down longer questions or tasks. Remember that these features won't appear in your actual assessment!

Grey boxes like this contain **hints and tips** about ways that you might complete a task, interpret a brief, understand a concept or structure your responses.

Guided This icon will appear next to an example partial answer to a revision question or task. You should read the partial answer carefully, then complete it in your own words.

This is a **revision activity**. It will help you understand some of the skills needed to complete the revision question or task.

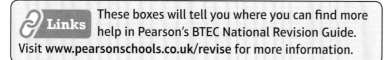

Links These boxes will tell you where you can find more help in Pearson's BTEC National Revision Guide. Visit www.pearsonschools.co.uk/revise for more information.

There is often space on the pages for you to write in. However, if you are carrying out research and making ongoing notes, you may want to use separate paper. Similarly, some units will be assessed through submission of digital files, or on screen, rather than on paper. Ask your tutor or check the Pearson website for the most up-to-date details.

Contents

Unit 2: Developing a Marketing Campaign

Unit 3: Personal and Business Finance

Unit 6: Principles of Management

Unit 7: Business Decision Making

A small bit of small print

Pearson publishes Sample Assessment Material and the Specification on its website. This is the official content and this book should be used in conjunction with it. The questions in this book have been written to help you practise the knowledge and skills you will require for your assessment. Remember: the real assessment may not look like this.

Unit 2: Developing a Marketing Campaign

Your assessment

Unit 2 will be assessed through a task, which will be set by Pearson. You will need to use your understanding of marketing to carry out independent research. Based on this, you will use your skills to produce a rationale and a budgeted plan for a marketing campaign.

Your Revision Workbook

This Workbook is designed to **revise skills** that might be needed in your assessed task. The details of your actual assessed task may change from year to year so always make sure you are up to date. Ask your tutor or check the **Pearson website** for the most up-to-date **Sample Assessment Material** to get an idea of the structure of your assessed task and what this requires of you.

To support your revision, this Workbook contains revision tasks to help you revise the skills that might be needed in your assessed task. The revision tasks are divided into sections.

Researching and making notes

In your Workbook you will use your skills to:

- carry out your own independent research of a given market
- make notes, including data such as facts and figures relating to organisations that produce or sell a particular product(s) and the ways they use the marketing mix in their promotional campaigns (pages 3–18).

Reviewing further information

You will then use your skills to:

- review further information about the given market (pages 19–20)
- use this and your preparatory notes to go on and respond to the activities.

Responding to activities

Your response to the activities will help you to revise:

- preparing a rationale for a marketing campaign based on a specific product(s), including:
  - marketing aims and objectives
  - research data on the market and competition
  - justification for your rationale (pages 21–28)
- developing a budgeted plan based on your rationale, with a timescale for your marketing campaign, and presenting it in an appropriate format to the owners of the organisation (pages 29–33).

Links To help you revise skills that might be needed in your Unit 2 set task, this Workbook contains two revision tasks, starting on pages 2 and 34. The first is guided and models good techniques, to help you develop your skills. The second gives you the opportunity to apply the skills you have developed. See the introduction on page iii for more information on features included to help you revise.

Revision task 1

To support your revision, the revision task below helps you revise the skills that might be needed in your assessed task. The revision task consists of two activities based on a task brief and your research notes.

The details of the actual assessed task may change so always make sure you are up to date. Ask your tutor or check the Pearson website for the most up-to-date Sample Assessment Material to get an idea of the structure of your assessed task and what this requires of you.

Revision task brief

- You are required to independently research the gym and fitness market.
- You should research and analyse at least one marketing campaign related to the gym and fitness market and its associated costs.
- You will need to prepare short notes that include facts and figures relating to organisations that offer gym and fitness facilities to members, including the products and services they offer, and the ways they use the marketing mix in their promotional campaigns.

In this Workbook you can refer to any notes you make with your research. In your actual assessment, you may not be allowed to refer to notes, or there may be restrictions on the length and type of notes that are allowed. Check with your tutor or look at the most up-to-date Sample Assessment Material on the Pearson website for information.

For this revision task, part of the research has been done for you. You will also need to carry out some of your own research. Have a look at pages 3–18 for an example of the sort of research notes you could make.

Don't be tempted to think of your research notes as the 'answers' to the activities in the revision task. View your notes as a 'tool' for identifying the key marketing principles you have studied. You will then be able to identify any gaps in your knowledge.

Researching and making notes

Writing your research notes

Before you start writing your research notes, you will need to spend time considering what you might need to know about the gym and fitness market and the type of information you could research. For example: Is the market growing? Who are the main producers? What products/services do they offer? What are their target markets? What media could a gym business use to market its products? What would be the cost of each method?

Your research may include:

- Primary and secondary data relating to:
  - organisations that offer gym and fitness classes and facilities to their members
  - market size, share and structure
  - trends
  - external influences.
- At least one marketing campaign related to the gym and fitness market, which should consider:
  - costs
  - timescales
  - media used
  - message communicated
  - marketing mix
  - appropriateness of the campaign.

Make a list of the data you might need to find out about the gym and fitness market. You will need at least six pieces of information. You might want to think about researching relevant information relating to the industry with regards to the size, growth, competition and consumers, e.g. what is the size of the industry?

Pages 3–18 are examples of the type of notes you could make as you research and gather information. Read and complete them carefully as you will use these notes to help you complete the activities, starting on page 21. Notice how the notes are structured with clear headings.

Market size, share, structure and trends

- Look at the market in the UK as a whole. You could then research your own area or region.
- You could also look at different sectors of the market, e.g. low cost or luxury.
- Use data and statistics, making a note of where the information is from.
- Look at what has happened recently, what has changed within the market and what has caused those changes.
- Make sure that you make a note of the sources used so you can refer to them in your work.
- Include website addresses so you can review them again later if you need to.
- Check your sources are reliable and the information is accurate.

What sources of information can you use to gather this information?

....

....

How do you know that a source or website is reliable?

....

....

How can you check that the information you have gathered is correct?

....

....

....

Guided

Market size, share, structure and trends

- Fitness industry now estimated to have market value of £4.3 billion, increased by 5.4% since last year. Total gym membership in the UK increased by 5.8% since last year.
- One in every eight people in the UK is a member of a gym and 13.7% of the UK population are registered as a member of a private health and fitness gym or a publicly owned fitness facility.
- There has been a 3.3% increase in the number of fitness facilities and 191 new public and private facilities opened in the last year.
- Over 1.5 million people in London are members of a gym and there are approximately 295 gyms and leisure centres in London.

Source: 'State of the UK fitness industry report', The Leisure Database Company Ltd http://www.leisuredb.com/2014-fitness-press-release

- Gym and fitness centres industry has a low level of market share concentration, as top four companies are estimated to account for just over 20% of the total industry revenue.
- Despite large companies such as Virgin Active, David Lloyd Clubs and Bannatyne Group having a strong presence in the market, there are a large number of small independent gyms operating across the UK.
- Established companies like Fitness First and LA Fitness have suffered from falling memberships and have had to close gyms. There has been an increase in the number of low-cost gyms in the UK, with this sector accounting for 24% of total membership in the UK.

Source: 'Gym & fitness centres in the UK: Market research report', IBIS World http://www.ibisworld.co.uk/market-research/gyms-fitness-centres.html

Don't just copy and paste facts into your notes. Make sure you understand what the information or data means and put it into your own words. For example, what is market share concentration? If you don't know what something means, find out!

Targeting markets and products

Guided

- Nearly four-fifths of UK adults have set themselves at least one health or fitness goal, yet only 12% currently use a gym.
- In London just 10% of the population are members of budget gyms, while in Frankfurt around half the city has signed up to local no-frills sites.

Source: 'The Gym Group proves that no-frills, pay-as-you-go gyms work out well', Independent http://www.independent.co.uk/news/business/analysis-and-features/the-gym-group-proves-that-no-frills-pay-as-you-go-gyms-work-out-well-a6727996.html

Primary research

You will need to undertake some primary research regarding the target market for gyms. You could start by creating a table similar to the one below and interviewing 10 people to establish some data. You may also feel it's appropriate to create a graph to summarise and analyse the data results.

Make sure you interview both males and females from a range of different age groups to provide you with relevant and valid data.

Gender	Age	Number of gym visits per week	Typical time of visits (am/pm/evening)	Length of typical visit	Duration of travel to gym	Key benefits of gym visits	Price of gym membership

Sectors and profiles

- Low-cost budget gyms now offer a 24/7 operation.
- This attracts a lot of shift-workers from across the social spectrum, from doctors and nurses to people who work behind a bar.

Source: Independent http://www.independent.co.uk/news/business/analysis-and-features/the-gym-group-proves-that-no-frills-pay-as-you-go-gyms-work-out-well-a6727996.html

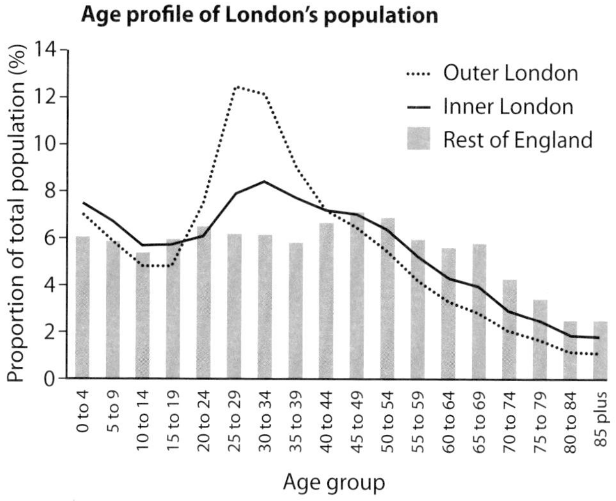

Source: Office for National Statistics, Mid-year population estimates, 2014 http://www.londonspovertyprofile.org.uk/indicators/topics/londons-geography-population/londons-population-by-age/

- What does the data tell you about potential customers for a gym?
- What does this mean for the gym business and its marketing campaigns?

....

....

....

Average salaries – profiling an area

Borough	Average salary
City of London, Kensington and Chelsea	£98 400
Wandsworth	£35 588
Richmond upon Thames	£34 505
Islington	£33 670
Hammersmith and Fulham	£32 485
Camden	£31 758
Tower Hamlets	£30 721
Bromley	£30 559
Waltham Forest	£23 700
Barking and Dagenham	£23 301
Enfield	£24 663
Croydon	£26 367
Westminster	£36 519
Barnet	£25 755
Ealing	£26 738
Lambeth	£28 764
Kingston upon Thames	£30 054

Source: ONS statistics from the LBC website, 20 November 2014 www.lbc.co.uk

Use the information in the table above to consider:

- the types of gym that might suit different profiles of salary
- the price of the gym membership that might be suitable for different salaries

Attendance profiles

Attendance over a day at a 'typical' club

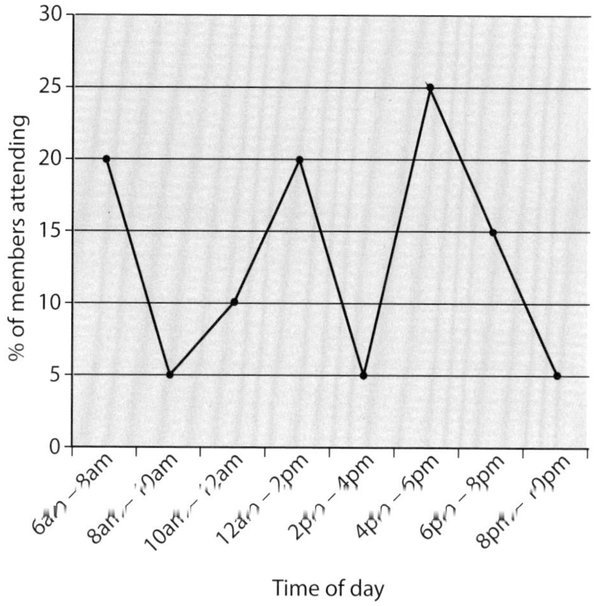

Attendance over a week at a 'typical' club

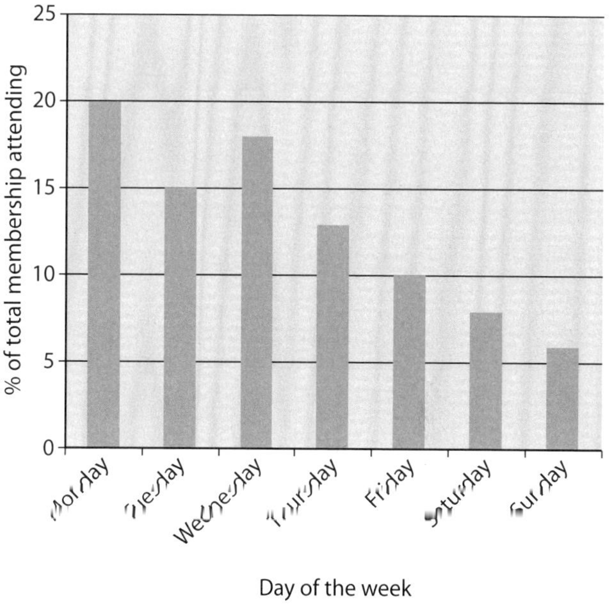

Source: PT Direct
http://www.ptdirect.com

Look at the data in the graphs above and write some notes to answer the following questions.

- What do the graphs tell you about demand from customers at different times of the day and the week?
- What would this mean for a gym business?
- How could the owner of a gym business use this information to help them plan?

....

....

....

Product availability and unique selling points

1. Consider the research notes and data so far. What might you need to consider when bringing together unique selling points for a gym and fitness business? List some examples.

....

....

....

....

2. Explain the stages of the product life cycle.

....

....

....

....

Links For more information on unique selling points see the Revision Guide, page 139. To revise the product life cycle, see the Revision Guide, page 17.

Guided

- There are a wide range of gyms and health clubs in the industry catering for different markets, including traditional gyms, women-only gyms, premium full-service health clubs, 24-hour gyms and budget models gyms.

Make sure you research the different types of gyms so you understand what they offer and how they work. You might want to find examples of gyms which fall into each category.

- Many gyms include other activities to boost revenue and maintain membership numbers, e.g.
- themed group classes like Zumba
- yoga
- boot camps
- mainstream sports such as five-a-side football, squash and badminton.

Source: Gym and fitness centres in the UK industry research report http:www.prweb.com/releases/2013/8/prweb10996477.htm

- Budget gyms now offering low prices, achieved by using cheaper sites without the luxuries of swimming pools, food and drink, spas and saunas.

Source: 'The Gym Group proves that no-frills, pay-as-you-go gyms work out well', *Independent* http://www.independent.co.uk/news/business/analysis-and-features/the-gym-group-proves-that-no-frills-pay-as-you-go-gyms-work-out-well-a6727996.html

- Traditional gyms offer a range of facilities including tennis courts, indoor and outdoor pools, gyms, sports shops and café bars, restaurants and beauty salons, crèches, etc.
- Price of gym membership varies depending on location and type of gym. Gym membership costs £15.99 a month at Fitness4less, a low-cost gym in East London, whereas Fitness First members pay up to £70 per month.

Source: *The Economist* http:www.economist.com/news/britain/21629530-cut-price-gyms

What does all this information tell you about the products available in the fitness and gym industry?

External influences

For social and economic factors, you will find it helpful to complete a PESTLE analysis. Give some examples of what you might include under each heading. The examples completed so far reflect the position in 2016.

Guided

External influences

POLITICAL

- The National Minimum Wage increased to £7.20 in April 2016 for those aged 25 and over.
- The UK voted to leave the European Union on 23 June 2016.

How do political factors impact on a gym and fitness business?

....

....

....

What can businesses do to respond?

....

....

....

ECONOMIC

- The UK economy is currently in the recovery stage of the economic cycle, with GDP increasing by 0.4% in the first quarter of 2016.
- The average income in the UK has risen to £26 500 in 2016.
- The UK inflation rate in June 2016 was 0.5%.
- In the second quarter of 2016, unemployment was 4.9%.

What key economic indicators do we use to judge the performance of the economy?

....

....

....

....

....

SOCIAL

- One motivation for joining a gym is to meet new people.
- Shift work and homeworking are common in the UK.
- On average, Britons work 43.6 hours per week.
- 25% of adults in England are obese and 62% of adults are overweight or obese.

How do social factors impact on a gym and fitness business?

....

....

....

What can businesses do to respond?

....

....

....

TECHNOLOGICAL

- A number of fitness apps have now been introduced to provide fitness programmes with a limited cost.
- Growth of the internet means that homeworking has become more common.

How do technological factors impact on a gym and fitness business?

....

....

....

What can businesses do to respond?

....

....

....

LEGAL

The Data Protection Act 1998 controls how businesses store and use customers' personal information.

Advertising codes of practice ensure that all advertising is honest and accurate.

The Trade Descriptions Act 1968 ensures that false or misleading information cannot be included in any advertising.

Direct debit regulations are in place to control how membership fees can be collected from members.

What laws control advertising practices and financial services?

....

....

....

....

....

....

....

Consider how each of the laws or regulations might impact on a gym or fitness business.

ENVIRONMENTAL

A congestion charge zone introduced in central London in 2003 aimed at reducing congestion and traffic in the city centre.

A level 7 pollution warning alert was placed on Central and West London in 2015, with the London Mayor advising people to spend less time outside to protect their health.

The 2011 census shows that there is overcrowding in Inner East and South London, with four boroughs being overcrowded by 30% or more.

How do environmental and ethical factors impact on a gym and fitness businesses?

....

....

....

What can businesses do to respond to these pressures?

....

....

....

Sources:
GOV.UK
Economics Online
Daily Mail
Public Health England, https://www.noo.org.uk/NOO_about_obesity/adult_obesity/UK_prevalence_and_trends
www.vistlondon.com
Evening Standard, http://www.standard.co.uk/news/health/boris-tells-londoners-to-spend-less-time-outdoors-to-improve-health-10113183.html
ONS

Consider the information a PESTLE analysis would result in for the gym and fitness market, and how each factor might inform considerations in a marketing campaign.

Links For support on how to carry out a PESTLE analysis, see the Revision Guide, page 19.

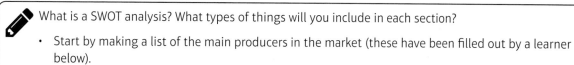

SWOT analysis of main producers

Guided

What is a SWOT analysis? What types of things will you include in each section?

- Start by making a list of the main producers in the market (these have been filled out by a learner below).
- Research each one, finding out what segment of the market they operate in, such as low-cost market.
- Find out how many outlets they have and where they are.
- Look at the products and services they offer.

Main producers:

David Lloyd Clubs – middle market

....

....

Fitness First – middle market

....

....

LA Fitness – middle market

....

....

Virgin Active – middle market

....

....

Bannatyne Group – middle market

....

....

The Gym Group – low-cost market

....

....

PureGym – low-cost market

....

....

Xercise4less – low-cost market

....

....

EasyGym – low-cost market

....

....

Links For further support on how to carry out a SWOT analysis, see the Revision Guide, page 19.

Guided

SWOT analysis of main producers

STRENGTHS

- The industry has low market share concentration, with four main companies accounting for just over 20% of industry revenue.
- Annual memberships increased from 12.6% to 13.2% in 2015 and the number of fitness facilities increased by 1.5%.
- Virgin Active and David Lloyd Clubs have both undertaken makeovers, with faster fitness feedback and more engagement with users.
- Fitness First have reintroduced better qualified personal trainers to provide more of a focus on health and wellbeing.

WEAKNESSES

- Virgin Active, David Lloyd Clubs and Bannatyne Group have opened new branches in the UK in recent years.
- David Lloyd Clubs, for example, have grown by 1.3% between 2011 and 2016, with an annual revenue of £2 billion, employing 39 585 employees.
- There is a rising number of mobile trainers and boot camps/outdoor fitness companies.
- Middle market producers now account for less than 50% of the market share of the total industry.
- There is a rise in very accessible and affordable mobile apps and fitness DVDs endorsed by celebrities that help people train in the comfort of their own home at a lower cost.

OPPORTUNITIES

- A wide range of gyms in the industry cater to different markets, allowing producers to specialise in different areas in the market. This includes women-only gyms, traditional gyms, premium full-service clubs, 24-hour gyms and budget gyms.
- Increased demand for gyms offering 24/7 services and pay-as-you-go services such as Xercise4Less and Pure Gym.
- The monthly charge for middle market gyms ranges between £21 and £49. Low-cost gyms have monthly fees as low as £5.

THREATS

- Growth and expansion of low-cost gyms such as The Gym Group, PureGym, easyGym and Xercise4Less, create challenges for the established middle market. Low-cost gyms now account for 23% of the market.
- There is also increased competition from a new generation of producers offering services on a pay-as-you-go basis for class-based concepts such as Psycle (spinning) and Barry's Bootcamp (high intensity workout).

Sources:
'The UK's health and fitness sector', Savills: http://www.savills.co.uk/research_articles/186866/186682-0/
Gym and fitness centres in the UK industry research report: http:www.prweb.com/releases/2013/8/prweb10996477.htm
Gym and fitness centres in the UK: Market research report, IBIS World: http://www.ibisworld.co.uk/market-research/gyms-fitness-centres.html

How might you use a SWOT analysis to identify competitor positioning and inform the design of a marketing plan?

Researching a marketing campaign

You will need to undertake your own research on costings.

Make a list of the forms of media a business could use to advertise its products.

Put them in order of estimated cost from the most expensive to the least expensive.

....

....

....

....

....

....

....

....

....

....

Guided

TV advertising campaigns

The following are examples of TV advertising packages:

Source: https://www.tvadvertising.co.uk/index.php?tv-advertising-costs

BRONZE	SILVER	GOLD
Bronze Package – £20 000 includes: • Production of a 30" advert • Clearing of a 30" advert • Playout to all TV station(s) on plan • Estimated 3.75m views of your 30" advert (National, Daytime) • Day to day planning, buying and monitoring of your TV campaign by our experienced buyers • Spot lists sent week before campaign starts, weekly updates & final spot list	Silver Package – £35 000 includes: • Production of a 30" advert • Clearing of a 30" advert • Playout to all TV station(s) on plan • Estimated 6.5m views of your 30" advert (National, Daytime) • Day to day planning, buying and monitoring of your TV campaign by our experienced buyers • Spot lists sent week before campaign starts, weekly updates & final spot list • Post campaign analysis – comparing actual delivery against planned delivery	Gold Package – £50 000 includes: • Production of a 30" advert • Clearing of a 30" advert • Playout to all TV station(s) on plan • Estimated 10m views of your 30" advert (National, Daytime) • Day to day planning, buying and monitoring of your TV campaign by our experienced buyers • Spot lists sent week before campaign starts, weekly updates & final spot list • Post campaign analysis – comparing actual delivery against planned delivery

- David Lloyd Clubs is an example of a competitor health club business which has used TV advertising campaigns as part of a marketing campaign to promote their clubs.

Source: http://www.lawcreative.co.uk/portfolio/david-lloyd-leisure/

Newspaper and magazine advertising

- David Lloyd Clubs has also used magazine advertising to promote their clubs.

Source: http://www.lawcreative.co.uk/portfolio/david-lloyd-leisure/

- It costs over £30 000 for a full-page colour advertisement in *The Daily Mail.*
- The cost of local newspapers can vary greatly: on average it costs in excess of £250 for a quarter-page advertisement.
- A full-page advertisement in a magazine with a readership of 5000 people will cost at least £200.

Source: Newspaper and magazine advertising costs, Marketing Minefield: http://www.marketingminefield.co.uk/print-advertising-costs/

> **Links** Make sure you consider the reliability and validity of your sources. For information on the reliability and validity of sources, see the Revision Guide, page 13.

- David Lloyd Clubs have a well-designed and professional website which is a key promotional tool for their business. The cost of setting up a website can range from £10 000 to £100 000 and as this is a high-quality website designed by a web design company, this would cost towards the highest price quoted. **Source:** http://webdesign.expertmarket.co.uk/how-much-does-website-cost

Social media

- The fastest and cheapest method of reaching customers/consumers but isn't always free so you may incur costs.
- Marketing consultants offer a range of social media support packages. A basic set-up fee for Facebook, Twitter and Google+ is around £150. The monthly management fee which includes two–three updates per day is around £250 per month.

Source: YogurtTop Marketing: www.yogurttopmarketing.co.uk/social-media/social-media-packages.php

Radio advertising

As a guide, a week-long campaign that uses a 30-second advert (minus production costs) could cost anything from:

- £500 on a local station
- £2500 on a regional station
- Upwards from £10 000 on a national station

Source: Radioadvertising.co.uk: http://www.radioadvertising.co.uk/costs

Outdoor advertising

- The average cost of outdoor advertising is around £200 per week for a standard 48-sheet billboard. An advert on the side of a bus stop on a busy high street could cost about £300 for two weeks' exposure.

Source: www.marketingdonut.co.uk

Leaflets

- David Lloyd Clubs have also produced leaflets to offer a free 7-day trial to their clubs, meaning that full revenue would not be generated over the 7-day trial period. This will mean that the club will be missing out on revenue over the 7 days of the trail. The leaflets are of a high quality – glossy and full colour – so may be more expensive than the price quoted by VistaPrint for individual customers (rather than a business-to-business model), which is 1000 leaflets from £19.99 excl. VAT.

> Consider other creative ways could you get your marketing messages across, that would be cost-effective and make an impact.

Example of a marketing campaign

Now you will need to research and analyse a marketing campaign of your choice. It should be related to the gym and fitness market. You might want to research a campaign run by one of the businesses listed on page 11, or you could research a campaign run by a local independent fitness business. Make notes on the campaign using the questions below to help you.

Links To revise marketing campaigns, see the Revision Guide, pages 31–33.

Title of marketing campaign:

....

Think about the rationale behind the campaign. Identify its aims and objectives, and how these relate to sales, brand recognition and brand awareness.

Explain the rationale for the campaign.

....

....

....

Links Revise marketing aims and objectives on pages 2–3 of the Revision Guide, and branding on page 6.

Brief description of product:

....

Identify the unique selling points and benefits of the product.

....

....

....

....

Identify the needs of the target market.

....

....

....

Links You can find out more about identifying what customers want in the Revision Guide, page 9.

Outline the campaign's marketing message.

....

....

Is the marketing message straightforward?
Does it clearly identify the target market?
Does it target the 'problem' faced by the market?
Does it provide a solution to the 'problem'?

Assess whether the marketing message sends a clear message to its target audience.

....

....

....

Links Revise marketing messages on page 28 of the Revision Guide.

Guided Describe the different elements of the marketing mix incorporated within the campaign.

Product: ....

....

....

Price: ....

....

....

Promotion: ....

....

....

Place: ....

....

....

Links Find out about the elements of the marketing mix and extended marketing mix on pages 21–27 of the Revision Guide.

If appropriate, consider the elements of the extended marketing mix.

People: ....

....

....

Physical environment: ....

....

....

Process: ....

....

....

Next, consider product factors such as functionality, styling, quality, safety and packaging. Is the pricing structure right? Is the product in the right place at the right time?

Discuss the decisions on product, price, promotion and place.

....

....

....

....

Identify the media used to advertise the campaign. Outline any other methods used to put across the message.

....

....

....

....

Discuss the balance of advertising, sales promotions, personal selling and public relations.

....

....

....

Assess whether the campaign captured the attention of the market.

....

....

Explain how the message was given credibility.

....

....

Outline the action the message wants the consumer to take.

....

....

Outline the timescale of the campaign.

....

....

Identify the associated costs of the campaign.

....

If you are unable to research an exact figure, try to assess the size of the campaign budget based on the types of media used.

Describe the ways in which the campaign has been monitored by the business.

....

....

Links Media and budgets are covered in the Revision Guide on page 29, and timelines and evaluation (monitoring) on page 30.

Finally, you need to evaluate the campaign. Re-read the notes you have made during your research and write down your own thoughts.

....

....

....

....

....

....

....

....

You may be allowed to take some of your preparatory notes into your supervised assessment time. If so, there may be restrictions on the length and type of notes that are allowed. Check with your tutor or look at the most up-to-date Sample Assessment Material on the Pearson website for information.

Reviewing further information

Read the information that follows about a gym and fitness business.

You will then tackle Revision activity 1 where you need to prepare a rationale for John's Gyms, including marketing aims and objectives, research data on the market and competition, and justify your rationale.

In Revision activity 2 you will go on to develop a budgeted plan with a timescale for a marketing campaign, presented in an appropriate format.

Start by underlining or highlighting key points in the information below that you could use in your activities, and make notes. The first paragraph about John's Gyms has been done for you.

The gym and fitness market

The UK gym and fitness market is growing again after struggling to maintain membership and market value during the recession since 2009. The UK fitness industry has grown by 5.4% in the past few years and the total market value is now estimated to be £4.3 billion. Today, one in every eight people in the UK is a member of a gym.

Over a 12-month period there has been positive growth, with increases of 5.4% in value, 3.3% in the number of fitness facilities and a 5.8% rise in the number of members.

The growth of the industry continues to be driven by strong performance from the rapidly growing low-cost market in the private sector. This expanding market now accounts for 9% of the total number of private clubs, 10% of the private market value and 24% of the private sector membership.

Increasing market share in the gym and fitness industry

The following information relates to John's Gyms, a medium-sized gym and fitness business. John is looking to expand the business by opening more outlets. You are required to prepare **both** a rationale **and** a budgeted plan for a marketing campaign for this business.

John's Gyms

John's Gyms is a gym and fitness business that was started in 1993 in Manchester. John initially opened one gym and fitness centre in the city centre, offering gym facilities and fitness classes for both men and women. The business has continued to grow and John now has ten gym and fitness centres across the north of England. The gym and fitness centres have been targeted towards people on middle incomes who work or live within city centres. The business continues to be successful, achieving sales turnover of £2.3 million last year. However, in the past few years, a number of other gym and fitness centres have entered the market alongside the other national chains of gyms already established as market leaders. These new gym and fitness centres are targeted towards the low-cost market and initial signs indicate that they have been successful in establishing market share in this sector of the market.

This gives you an indication of John's Gyms target market and tells you that the marketing campaign needs to appeal to both men and women.

This tells you that John's Gyms are well established in the north of England and therefore it is a regional business.

Again this tells you about the business's target market and therefore your marketing campaign needs to be targeted towards middle-income city dwellers.

This tells you that the business is medium in size and is relatively successful in the area of the market in which they operate. It also gives you an indication of the aims of the business in terms of sales revenue and this can be used to help you develop John's Gyms' marketing aims and objectives.

This tells you that the fitness and gym market is becoming more competitive and that John's Gyms is going to face more competitors as it starts to expand.

This tells you that the market has changed and competitors have entered the market, offering cheaper gym memberships.

Guided

You need to understand the terms used in the task information. Make some notes to help you to remember what they mean. One term is already defined below.

Sales turnover – this is the money made from selling your product or service.

....

....

....

....

....

....

John is now looking to expand his business, initially by opening three new gym and fitness centres in London. These gym and fitness centres will offer gym facilities and fitness classes, alongside a shop which will sell fitness products, and a café, offering healthy snacks, drinks and food. John plans to have the first gym and fitness centre up and running in six months' time. John has set a marketing budget of £150 000 initially, and there is scope for this to increase if the campaign proves successful.

John offers yearly and monthly membership packages for the gym. This includes access to the gym, swimming pool and changing facilities. He plans to offer a range of fitness classes, and there will be an additional cost for each class, although members can sign up for classes in advance, when paying for their membership, at a reduced rate. Personal training will also be available at an additional cost and the personal trainer at each gym is also keen to offer boot camps in local parks.

Look again at the final two paragraphs of the task information above and repeat the underlining process yourself. For each section you underline, explain in a sentence what it tells you about the business. You can make notes by the paragraphs and below. You may find this technique helps you to understand how to use the information provided.

....

....

....

....

....

....

....

....

Responding to activities

To answer the two revision questions you will have carried out research into the gym and fitness market (pages 2–18) and reviewed further information (pages 19–20).

In this Workbook you may refer to any notes you have made as you respond to the activities. In your actual assessment you may not be allowed to use your preparatory notes, or there may be restrictions on the length and type of notes that are allowed. Check with your tutor or look at the latest Sample Assessment Material on the Pearson website for details.

Revision activity 1

Prepare a rationale for the marketing campaign for John's Gyms. This should include:

- marketing aims and objectives
- research data on the market and competition
- justification for your rationale.

Complete the response to Revision activity 1 below, using the guidance to support you.

Summary of marketing campaign's rationale

Here you need to outline the marketing campaign's rationale. This should include any background information you have on John's Gyms and what this means for the marketing campaign. Use the information on pages 19–20 and from your research to help you do this.

Consider:

- What is John's Gyms aiming to achieve? It would be useful to identify what the overall aims and objectives are in order to set appropriate marketing aims and objectives.
- What sector of the industry does John's Gyms currently operate in? Who are their customers?
- At what stages in the product life cycle are John's Gyms products?
- What is happening in the industry in general? What has changed? How will this affect John's Gyms and its marketing campaign?
- What are your initial ideas and plans for the marketing campaign?

Guided John can use product, promotion, pricing and place to help him structure his marketing plan:

Links Revise the **marketing mix** on pages 21–26 of the Revision Guide.

Product

....

....

....

....

....

Promotion

....

....

....

....

....

Pricing

....

Place

....

Remember to use the correct marketing terminology.

Create a glossary of important terms for this unit.

....

Marketing aims and objectives

Links For support with the marketing aims and objectives, see the Revision Guide, pages 2–3.

In this section you need to be clear about what you are aiming to achieve, and the purpose of your campaign. Try to include at least four objectives but you can include more if you want to. Remember: Your aims and objectives should be SMART.

Write down the meaning of SMART. Practise writing some SMART targets for yourself before you write them for John's Gyms.

For each objective, clearly state what the planned outcome of the marketing activity will be and how the business will plan to achieve this. It would also be useful to make a note of why the objective is appropriate for John's Gyms, as this will help you to complete your justification for your rationale later.

Guided

Marketing aims and objectives

John's Gyms has clear marketing aims and objectives:

Objective 1

Inform target audience about features and benefits of John's Gyms within six months.

Objective 2

Objective 3

Objective 4

....

....

....

....

Objective 5

....

....

....

....

Links For information on SMART objectives, see the Revision Guide, page 18.

Research data on the market and competition

You should outline the main findings of your research. This means focusing on the target market and the competition. It would be useful to use headings to help you organise your work. There are some suggested headings provided below.

Have a look at the research notes on pages 3–18 to complete this part of the response. Remember to say why the research is reliable and valid.

Each of the sections below has been started to help you. Read the information provided and then complete the section yourself.

Guided

The market, size, structure and trends

To research into the fitness and gym market I firstly used the 'State of the UK fitness industry report' produced by The Leisure Database Company Ltd. This report says that the fitness and gym market is worth £4.3 billion in the UK and has increased by 5.4% in the past year. This is an important piece of research as it demonstrates that the market is growing at a healthy rate and therefore there is room for John's Gyms to expand further.

....

....

....

....

....

....

The target market

Nearly four-fifths of UK adults have set themselves at least one fitness goal, but only 12% currently use a gym. This means that there is demand for fitness products as people are concerned about their level of fitness. John's Gyms needs to find a way to encourage these people as only 12% of adults actually visit a gym. This is important information as John needs to know that there is a need for his gym or he will not be successful. Also, he needs to be aware that people don't always go to the gym even if they need to.

....

....

....

....

....

....

....

....

Affordability

My research into the economy using the GOV.UK website has shown average incomes in the UK rose to £26 500 in 2016. This means that on average people have more money to spend and, as John's Gyms are targeted at people with middle incomes, this means that they have more potential customers for their gyms. This tells me that John's Gyms' expansion has the potential to be successful. This is an important piece of research as John's Gyms need to know that people have enough money to afford their gym membership.

Competition

My research using the Savills report on 'The UK's health and fitness sector' shows that there has been a growth in low-cost gyms such as The Gym Group and Xercise4less. This sector now accounts for 23% of the market. This is very important to John's Gyms as the business is operating in the middle market of the gym industry and therefore will not be competing with these new gyms. However, he needs to be aware that this part of the industry is growing and it may take away some of his customers if people do not have much money.

Evaluation of the reliability and validity of the information research

Your evaluation of the reliability and validity of the information researched should outline the strengths or weaknesses of the sources used and a judgement of how reliable and valid the information researched is.

As the 'State of the UK fitness industry report' is a published report produced by a professional research company, the information is reliable and can be trusted and it provides valid information for John's Gym. Similar information was also provided in the task information and therefore this demonstrates that the information is accurate as it has been found in two different sources.

The GOV.UK website is a reliable and valid source of information as it is the government's website and it must ensure that the information provided is accurate.

The 'The UK's health and fitness sector' report is reliable and valid as it has been produced by Savills, who are a recognised research company.

....

....

....

....

....

....

....

....

Remember to include an overall judgement on how valid and reliable the sources of information you have used are.

Links To find out more about the importance of reliability and validity, see the Revision Guide, page 13.

Justification for my rationale

Here you will need to justify your rationale. This involves giving reasons for the decisions you have made. This should include:

- How do the aims and objectives of the marketing campaign relate to John's business and its overall aims and objectives?
- What is the target market for the business? How does this reflect the industry and recent trends?
- What does your research indicate for your marketing campaign?
- What are your initial ideas for your marketing campaign? How do you know they are the right things to do?

....

....

....

....

....

....

....

....

....

....

....

....

Revision activity 2

Based on the rationale you prepared for Revision activity 1, develop a budgeted plan with a timescale for your marketing campaign. You need to present this in a format appropriate to John's Gyms.

> Now write your response to Revision activity 2, using the guidance below to support you. Make sure your marketing campaign meets the marketing aims and objectives of John's Gyms that you outlined in Revision activity 1. You need to present this in a format appropriate to John's Gyms.
>
> Focus your marketing campaign on John's Gyms' target market.
>
> Take care to structure and present your response clearly. Think about:
> - The marketing mix
> - The marketing message
> - Budget and costs
> - Selection of media
> - Timescale
>
> Remember to use appropriate marketing terminology.
>
> In this Workbook, you should present your plan in the format of a formal report that could be read by the owner of John's Gyms. Your report should be clearly structured. If you wish, you could use word-processing software to complete the activity.

Guided

The marketing mix

Product development:

> Here you will need to outline the product. Make sure you read the information on pages 19–20 again before starting to write your response.
> - What will John's Gyms offer in their membership?
> - Are there additional services that John's Gyms will offer?
> - What form of branding will you use for John's Gyms?
> - How does this link to the other aspects of the marketing mix?
>
> Make sure you describe exactly what the product is and why this is appropriate to John's Gyms.

....

....

....

....

....

....

Pricing strategies:

Here you will need to outline the price of the gym membership and how this has been decided upon.

- What price is the gym membership? Make sure this will allow John to make profit.
- What other services will you charge for?
- What strategy has been used to decide on the price? (Penetration, skimming, competitor-based, cost-plus?)
- How does this compare to the competitors?
- How does this link to the other aspects of the marketing mix?

Remember to explain why the pricing structure is appropriate for John's Gyms.

....

....

....

....

....

....

....

....

....

....

Promotion and selection of media:

Here you should outline how you will use different media to promote John's Gyms. It is important to include a timescale and costings.

For each form of media used you need to explain:

- A description of the media used, e.g. what is the media, when will it be used, where, how often?
- Why did you choose this form and how is it appropriate for John's Gyms?
- What is the timescale of the promotion used?
- What is the cost?
- Why is it better than other forms of media?

....

....

....

....

....

Place:

- Where will the gyms be located? What size will they be?
- Why have you chosen this location? (Remember to think about your target market.)
- Will all the services on offer take place at the gym or will John use other locations such as local parks?
- Consider how expensive locations will be and if John can afford it.

Extended marketing mix:

Consider how you could use the extended marketing mix:
- People – How will you recruit the right staff? How will you ensure good customer service?
- Physical environment – How will you make the gyms attractive to your target market? Is there parking available? Are they easy to reach by public transport?
- Process – How will you make signing in and registering for other services efficient and cost effective?

Budget:

Here outline the amount of budget used and how it has been spent.
It is a good idea to set aside some of the budget as a contingency fund in case something goes wrong.

Timescale:

You will also need to consider the timescale. How long will it take to plan and then run the marketing campaign?

Evaluation:

Explain how you will know the marketing campaign will be successful. Link back to the marketing aims and objectives.

Revision task 2

To support your revision, the revision task below helps you revise the skills that might be needed in your assessed task. The revision task consists of two activities based on a task brief and your research notes.

The details of the actual assessed task may change so always make sure you are up to date. Ask your tutor or check the Pearson website for the most up-to-date Sample Assessment Material to get an idea of the structure of your assessed task and what this requires of you.

Revision task brief

- You are required to independently research the toys and games market.
- You should research and analyse one marketing campaign related to the toys and games market and its associated costs.
- You will need to prepare short notes that include facts and figures relating to organisations that produce or sell toys and games such as the products they offer and the ways they use the marketing mix in their promotional campaigns.

In this revision Workbook you can refer to any notes you make with your research. In your actual assessment, you may not be allowed to refer to notes, or there may be restrictions on the length and type of notes that are allowed. Check with your tutor or look at the most up-to-date Sample Assessment Material on the Pearson website for information.

Researching and making notes

For this revision task you will need to carry out your own research, but some hints and tips will be provided for you.

Look back at the notes in Revision task 1 to remind yourself how to prepare them. You will need to use additional paper to write out all your notes, or you may word process them if you prefer. Remember that you must include both primary and secondary research in your research notes.

Reading further information

Read the information that follows about Henderson's Toys.

You will then tackle Revision acitvity 1, where you need to prepare a rationale for the Henderson's Toys marketing campaign, including marketing aims and objectives, research data on the market and competition, and justify your rationale. In Revision activity 2 you will go on to develop a budgeted plan with a timescale for a marketing campaign, presented in an appropriate format.

Start by underlining or highlighting key points in the information below that you could use in your activities. Then research and make notes. You could use the approach taken in Revision task 1 to guide you. Where relevant, you could also use some of the key information and sources used in Revision task 1.

The toys and games market

The toys and games market in the UK is facing challenging conditions. While the total UK market is worth £5.7 billion, this has declined by 0.3% in the past five years. The market has faced fierce competition from foreign-made toys and games, which offer a cheaper alternative to UK-manufactured traditional toys. Asia now accounts for 28% of global sales.

Boys account for 55% of toys and games sales, with girls only making up 45% of all sales. The UK has the second highest spend on toys in the world, with UK parents spending on average £508 on toys per child each year. Middle-class households are very important to the toys and games industry because they largely drive consumer spending.

In recent years there has been a change in the type of toys and games sold, with video games now generating £2.52 billion in sales in 2015. Toys based on characters from films such as *Frozen* and *The Lego Movie* have remained popular in the market.

Rebranding in the toys and games market

Henderson's Toys is a toys manufacturer and retailer based in Harrogate in Yorkshire. The business is a family owned and run company which was established in 1873 by Henry Henderson and shares in the business have been passed down through the family ever since. George and Alison Henderson are now the main shareholders of the company, with nine other family members holding seats on the Board of Directors. Henderson's Toys make traditional toys: the range includes handmade teddy bears, dolls and wooden toys. The toys are well designed and use high-quality materials to ensure that the toys are well made. Alison Henderson has been the toys' designer for the past 30 years and the designs and specifications have changed little during this time. The toys are targeted towards middle- and high-income families.

Over the past ten years, Henderson's Toys has seen a steady decline in sales and in 2015 the company's sales turnover was £1.2 million. Many of the company's suppliers have increased their prices by between 10% and 15%. In addition, a local toy shop has decided to stock toys imported from a company in Asia which are on average 20% cheaper than Henderson's Toys' brands. The Board of Directors are concerned that the future is challenging for the company and have decided to undergo a rebranding exercise to try and relaunch their toys onto the UK market.

The company has set aside a marketing budget of £75 000 to relaunch the company's products to the UK market. They have decided to focus on their core bestselling products of handmade teddy bears, dolls and wooden toys. They are keen to remain as a high-quality brand, aimed at the middle- and higher-income markets. They have also had an increase in sales to the adult market recently and would like to focus on this aspect of the business, as well as maintaining their sales to parents of 2–8-year-olds.

Revision activity 1

Prepare a rationale for the Henderson's Toys marketing campaign.

This should include:

- Marketing aims and objectives
- Research data on the market and competition
- Justification for your rationale

Complete your work in the space provided.

Start with a summary of the marketing campaign's rationale.

Now identify Henderson's Toys' marketing aims and objectives.

Henderson's Toys can use the marketing mix – product, promotion, pricing and place – to help them structure their marketing plan.

To improve your response, make sure you mention the extended marketing mix and how this could help as a key part of the marketing campaign.

In this section, you will need to outline the main findings of your research. This means focusing on the target market and the competition. You could use sub-headings to help organise your answer:

- The market size, share, structure and trends
- Target market and products
- External influences
- SWOT analysis of main producers
- Researching a marketing campaign, including costings.

Include here an evaluation of the reliability and validity of the information researched. You will need to outline the strengths or weaknesses of the sources used and come to an overall judgement about the reliability of your research.

Finally, write a justification for your rationale.

Budget: Outline how much has been spent and on what. Consider whether this is in budget and what contingency is left over.

Timescale: How long will it take to plan and then run the marketing campaign?

Finally, you need to evaluate the marketing campaign. Explain how you will assess whether it is a success. Link back to the marketing aims and objectives.

Unit 3: Personal and Business Finance

Your assessment

Unit 3 will be assessed through an exam, which will be set by Pearson. You will need to apply your knowledge and understanding of personal and business finance to different business situations through your response to short factual questions and more in-depth questions.

Your Revision Workbook

This Workbook is designed to **revise skills** that might be needed in your exam. The details of your actual exam may change from year to year so always make sure you are up to date. Ask your tutor or check the **Pearson website** for the most up-to-date **Sample Assessment Material** to get an idea of the structure of your exam and what this requires of you. Make sure you check the instructions in relation to taking a calculator into the exam, and notice the number of marks given for questions on business finance and on personal finance.

To support your revision, this Workbook contains revision questions to help you revise the skills that might be needed in your exam.

Revision questions

Your response to the questions will help you to revise:

- The importance of managing personal finance
- The personal finance sector
- The purpose of accounting
- Understanding the purpose of accounting
- Selecting and evaluating different sources of business finance
- Using break-even analysis and cash flow forecasts
- Completing statements of comprehensive income and financial position and evaluating a business's performance

Question types

Questions are included that require short factual answers and more in-depth answers where you apply your knowledge in different situations. You will be given scenarios that provide background to a question or group of questions that relate to it. Some questions require calculations based on business data where you need to show your workings, so you will need a calculator.

The questions use the following types of command words:

Describe	Explain	Give	Identify	Outline	Illustrate
Analyse	Assess	Calculate	Discuss	Evaluate	

Links To revise command words, see page 81 of the Revision Guide.

Links To help you revise skills that might be needed in your exam this Workbook contains two sets of revision questions, starting on pages 45 and 64. The first is guided and models good techniques, to help you develop your skills. The second gives you the opportunity to apply the skills you have developed. See the introduction on page iii for more information on features included to help you revise.

Revision test 1

This Workbook is designed to revise skills that might be needed in your exam. The details of your actual exam may change from year to year so always make sure you are up to date. Ask your tutor or check the Pearson website for the most up-to-date Sample Assessment Material to get an idea of the structure of your exam and what this requires of you.

Section A: Personal finance

Answer ALL revision questions in the spaces provided.

The ability to handle and control money is an important skill to ensure personal and business success.

1 Give **two** functions of money.

This is a factual recall question. There are four possible correct responses – you only need to identify two functions.

Guided

(i) Means of exchange – can be used to buy, sell and trade goods and services.

(ii) ....

Links To revise the main functions of money, see page 45 in the Revision Guide.

Total for Question 1 = 2 marks

2 Describe how a pawnbroker works.

You need to provide a brief summary of the role of the pawnbroker. Write two to three sentences that clearly relate to each other. Think about the financial service offered by the pawnbroker and how this service is paid for.

....

....

....

Links You can find out about the role of the pawnbroker on page 55 of the Revision Guide.

Total for Question 2 = 2 marks

Guided

3 Explain **two** effects on borrowers if the interest rate increases.

Note down the points you want to include and then work out how to link them together. Complete the notes below.

Bank of England raises interest rates → Cost of borrowing rises

Immediate effect for borrowers →

....

....

Possible long-term consequences for borrowers →

....

....

....

First, define the key terms – what is meant by an increase in interest rates. Then link together the facts in a logical order, explaining how one factor can influence another and, where appropriate, provide a conclusion. Remember to use business terminology.

(i) When the Bank of England raises interest rates, the cost of borrowing will rise. It will ....

....

....

....

....

(ii) Faced by higher borrowing costs, borrowers ....

....

....

....

....

Total for Question 3 = 4 marks

Banking technology is changing at a rapid pace. Traditional ways of handling money such as cash and cheques and providing services to customers at local branches are no longer sufficient. Customers want instant access to their money and flexible 24/7 banking services.

Guided

4 Discuss why it is important for the customer to have access to the latest banking technologies.

List the main technologies that are available and then consider why these are important to customers and how it would affect them if they were not available.

Telephone banking – 24/7 automated service for simple transactions: checking balance, paying bills; customers can talk directly to an adviser

....

....

Online banking –

....

....

Mobile banking –

....

....

'Discuss' questions require you to consider different aspects of a topic, how they link together and their importance in order to give a balanced point of view.

You should look at both the advantages and disadvantages concerning the use of technology in banking. When answering, you may wish to consider the following areas:

- Convenience
- Transfers
- Security breaches for both the customer and the bank
- Speed
- Compatibility with other computer software
- Control

For personal customers, the use of the latest banking technologies offers ....

....

....

....

....

....

....

....

....

....

For business customers, electronic banking has many advantages. ....

....

The main disadvantages ....

....

Links Revise banking services and ways to pay on pages 48–49 and customer communication on page 56 of the Revision Guide.

Total for Question 4 = 6 marks

Over the past few years there has been increasing focus on individuals saving for their future needs. With low interest rates savers are looking for good deals.

Guided

5 Assess the use of ISAs as a method of saving.

What are the main advantages and disadvantages of ISAs?

....

'Assess' questions require you to weigh up the positive and negative aspects of a topic or situation and give your conclusion. You will need to consider both the advantages and the disadvantages of ISAs and compare these to other methods of saving that are available. Think about the return on your investment, accessibility and the safety of your investment.

An ISA is an Individual Savings Account which does not charge individuals tax on the interest earned on their savings, unlike other deposit or savings accounts where tax may be payable on the interest. There are two types of ISA:

....

....

....

....

....

....

....

....

....

....

....

....

....

....

....

....

....

....

....

....

Links For more on savings and ISAs, see the Revision Guide, page 52.

Total for Question 5 = 10 marks

Eleni has asked for advice on choosing a suitable motor insurance premium.

She has recently left college and has secured an accounting apprenticeship in a business located 25 miles from her home.

She has purchased a second-hand car for £1100.

This table gives the top five third party, fire and theft insurance quotations Eleni has found.

Table 1: Third party, fire and theft motor insurance quotations

Insurance company	Annual premium	Excess	Windscreen cover	Courtesy car in the event of accident repairs	Breakdown cover
Stockbridge Insurance	£1250	Compulsory £700 Voluntary £500	Included £60 excess	Not included	£60
United Insurers	£1330 12 monthly payments of £120	Compulsory £400 Voluntary £500	Included £50 excess	£15 per day	£55
Carterton plc	£1356	Compulsory £350 Voluntary £500	Included £45 excess	Included	£35
Rutland Cars	£1440 12 monthly payments of £120	Compulsory £300 Voluntary £500	Included £30 excess	£12 per day	£50
Cranford Insurance	£1884 12 monthly payments of £162	Compulsory £300 Voluntary £500	Included	Included	£50

6 Evaluate which of the motor insurance policies would be most suitable for Eleni.

Number the insurance companies 1–5 (1 being the best premium) for each of the quotations shown in the table and then judge which motor insurance policy has the best results overall.

....

....

....

....

....

....

....

....

....

'Evaluate' questions require you to reach a reasoned judgement from your own assessment of a set of alternatives.

Systematically work through the five different insurance quotations. You will need to focus on the annual cost and take account of the excesses and costs of any additional cover offered.

Total for Question 6 = 12 marks

END OF SECTION TOTAL FOR SECTION A = 36 MARKS

Section B: Business finance

Answer ALL revision questions. Write your answers in the spaces provided.

Howard Jakeman is the chairman of Rumsmeade United, a semi-professional football club. Howard runs the club with five full-time employees. They rely on match day income to pay their players and cover the running costs of the club.

You have been hired by Howard to help him with the financial side of the business.

Like all businesses, the football club incurs day-to-day running costs. It also has intangible assets.

7 Identify **two** types of revenue expenditure.

There are several possible correct responses to this question which simply requires you to recall facts. You need to provide only two examples of the day-to-day costs of running a business.

Guided

(i) Wages paid to the players and full-time employees

(ii) ....

Links You can find out about revenue expenditure in the Revision Guide, page 62.

Total for Question 7 = 2 marks

Guided

8 Outline what is meant by intangible assets.

Once you have defined intangible assets, apply your knowledge to the business scenario: what type of intangible assets might Rumsmeade United Football Club have?

These are non-physical capital items ....

....

....

....

Links Intangible assets are part of capital expenditure – see the Revision Guide, page 61.

Total for Question 8 = 2 marks

Howard has worked out that the average attendance is 996 for each game. Adults pay £13 and concessions are £7. The club plays 23 home league fixtures each season.

Guided

9 (a) Calculate the gross profit figure for a typical home league fixture. Assume that 25% of the tickets are sold to concessions. Show your workings. **5 marks**

Gross profit = Net sales – Cost of goods sold

First, you need to find out how many tickets are sold at the full price and how many at the concession rate. You can work out the number of tickets that will be concessions by dividing the total attendance by 4.

$\frac{996}{4}$ = ...

Now you know that 249 tickets will be concessions, you can subtract 249 from 996 to give you the total number of full price tickets.

996 – 249 = £..........

Multiply the total number of full price tickets by the ticket price of £13.

Total no. of full price tickets × £13 = £..........

Multiply the total number of concessionary tickets by the reduced ticket price of £7.

Total no. of concessionary tickets × £7 = £..........

Add these two totals together to calculate the gross profit figure.

Total income from full price tickets £.......... + total income from concessions £.......... = Gross profit £11454.

Links Find out more about gross profit in the Revision Guide, page 76.

(b) Calculate the home fixture gross profit for the season. Six additional home fixtures are cup games, with an average attendance of 1240. Show your workings. **8 marks**

First, you need to multiply the match day income by the number of games in the season to get the total income from the league games.

Total income from league games = number of home fixtures in the season ...23... × gross profit £.................... = £....................

Now you need to account for the total income from the cup games. First work out concessions (i.e. $\frac{1240}{4}$) and then follow the same calculations as for (a) i.e.:

Total number of full price tickets = total attendance 1240 – total number of concessions .... = ...

Income from full price tickets = total no. of full price tickets .... × £13 = £...............

Income from concessionary tickets = total no. of concessionary tickets .... × £7 = £..........

Gross profit = total income from full price tickets £.............. + Total income from concessions £.............. = £..............

Now multiply the gross profit by six (i.e. the number of home fixtures in the cup) to work out the total income from the cup games.

Gross profit £.................... × 6 = £....................

Finally add the total income from the league games to the total income from the cup games.

Total income from league games £.................... + total income from cup games £.................... = £349 002

On match day, the club's famous pies are sold in the ground and at given locations outside the ground. They are extremely popular. Each of the pies is sold for £2.

Table 2: Pies information

	Lamb £	Beef £	Chicken £	Vegetarian £	Total £
Revenue	900	1200	700	700	3500
Ingredients	150	250	100	100	600
Other variable costs	150	250	120	100	620
Contribution	600	700	480	500	2280
Fixed overheads					1040
Profit					1240

(c) Which of the four products gives the biggest contribution per unit? Show your workings.

4 marks

In each case, you need to divide the contribution by the revenue total.

Lamb = $\frac{600}{900}$ = £0.67

Beef = ...

Chicken = ...

Vegetarian= ....

Biggest contribution per unit ....

(d) What is the average contribution per unit across the four products? Show your workings.

2 marks

To calculate the mean average, add together the contribution per unit of each of the four products, and divide by the number of products (four).

Average contribution = ...

....

....

....

....

....

Links To calculate the break-even point of a product, you first need to work out the contribution per unit – the selling price per unit less the variable costs per unit. For support on break-even, see the Revision Guide, page 70. You will need to be able to calculate this for the next question.

Total for Question 9 = 19 marks

The club raises extra funds by printing replica sports shirts each year. The printing shop has a maximum capacity of 10 000 units. It has fixed costs of £12 000. The selling price of the shirts is £8 each. The variable cost per unit is £4.

Guided

10 (a) Calculate whether a profit or a loss has been made if the club sells 8000 sports shirts. Show your workings. **3 marks**

To work out the total costs you need to add the fixed costs to the variable costs on 8000 sports shirts.

Total costs = Fixed costs + (£4 × 8000) = £44 000

To work out the total income multiply the selling price by 8000.

Total income = selling price × 8000 = £64 000

Finally subtract the total costs from the total revenue.

Revenue − Total costs = £.............. profit

(b) Calculate the break-even point for the print shop operation. Show your workings. **2 marks**

Remember the formula:
Break-even point = Fixed costs/Contribution per unit

Fixed costs = £12 000

Variable costs = £4 per unit

Revenue per unit = £8

Therefore:

Contribution per unit = ...

Break-even point = ...

.... units need to be sold for the print shop to break even.

Total for Question 10 = 5 marks

Howard tells you that the club has £23 000 in a deposit account. They have agreed to sell part of the car park to a developer for £92 000.

Howard needs to raise £150 000 to buy a 99-year lease on the football ground from the local council.

Guided

11 Discuss ways that Howard could raise the remaining funds from external sources of finance.

Howard needs to raise £35 000 to ensure the club has sufficient funds to buy the lease. Complete the list of external sources of finance he could investigate to meet the shortfall.

Owner's capital

'Discuss' questions require you to consider different aspects of a topic, how they link together and their importance in order to give a balanced point of view.

There are several finance options that would be relevant in this case. These include: owner's capital, loans, crowd-funding, mortgage, venture capital, peer to peer lending, donations.

Think about the suggested methods and the reasons why some might be more easily attainable by the club. Also consider why the remaining methods may pose more problems and risks for the club if they chose them.

Links For sources of external finance available to businesses, see the Revision Guide, pages 64–65.

Total for Question 11 = 6 marks

The club has used some of its cash reserves to purchase a second-hand coach for £8000 to take players to away games. The plan is to use the coach for four years, when it will be disposed of for an estimated £500.

For the next two years, the club has negotiated a contract with a local sports club which will hire the coach for four days per week.

The club's accountant uses the straight-line method to account for depreciation.

Guided **12** Analyse the implications of the purchase of the coach on the club's financial statements.

You need to consider the items that are included in the statement of comprehensive income and the statement of financial position. The purchase of the coach increases the club's non-current assets but its cash reserves (current assets) have been reduced. The football club has to budget for additional expenses in the form of running costs of the coach (fuel, road tax, MOT and maintenance costs). The hire contract with the local sports club will generate additional income.

The club has to account for the depreciation of this non-current asset using the straight-line depreciation method.

Assets are shown in the statement of financial position, whereas additional income, expenses and depreciation are shown in the statement of comprehensive income of which the profit and loss account is a part.

Since the question provides financial data, you could use some of this information as part of your analysis – for example, by calculating the rate of depreciation over the four-year period using the straight-line method of depreciation.

The statement of comprehensive income sets out the business's revenue and expenses. ....

....

....

....

....

....

....

....

....

The club's statement of financial position records what the club is owed (its assets) and owes (its liabilities). ....

....

....

....

....

....

....

....

....

....

....

....

....

....

....

....

....

....

....

....

Links Depreciation is used to show the fall in value of machinery, office equipment and vehicles over time in the business's accounts. For support on straight-line and reducing-balance depreciation, see the Revision Guide, page 75.

Total for Question 12 = 8 marks

Howard has been considering the long-term future of the club. He has decided to use his own capital to cover the £35 000 shortfall needed to buy the 99-year lease. The only problem is that the club will not have any reserves left and this concerns him.

13 Assess the chances of Howard being able to attract venture capital to fund the club's expansion.

What is venture capital? How do you attract it? Who provides it? What are its main advantages and disadvantages?

....

....

....

....

....

....

....

....

....

....

'Assess' questions require you to weigh up the positive and negative aspects of a topic or situation and give your conclusion.

Outline what a venture capitalist or organisation would be looking for. This is a balance of risk and reward. They would be looking for potential growth, increased profits and an increase in the value of their investment over time.

Venture capital can be a long-term investment. It is committed share capital designed to help the business succeed. Howard would need to find someone who is prepared to have a longer term association with the club.

In the short to medium term he might be able to attract venture capital, but at a loss of control of some of the decision making and there might be pressure to sell some of the assets for short-term rewards.

....

....

....

....

....

....

....

....

....

....

....

Total for Question 13 = 10 marks

As part of his annual review of the club's activities Howard has calculated the following financial ratios on the club shop's activities. He wants to know if the shop is performing better than last year.

	Last year	**This year**
Gross profit margin	44%	41%
Net profit margin	13%	12%
ROCE	3%	3.5%
Current ratio	1.2:1	1.3:1
Liquid capital ratio	0.81:1	0.83:1
Trade receivable days	40	42
Trade payable days	36	34

Howard is hoping that the club shop will continue to provide a good source of income.

Guided

14 Evaluate the club shop's financial position using the data included in the table.

Businesses use ratios and other calculations to measure how well they are performing. What might each of the following ratios or calculations tell the business about its performance?

- Gross profit margin

....

- Net profit margin

....

- ROCE

....

- Current ratio

....

- Liquid capital ratio

....

- Trade receivable days

....

- Trade payable days

....

'Evaluate' questions require you to come to a reasoned judgement from your own assessment of a set of alternatives.

This particular question asks you to interpret or evaluate the information that has been provided. No calculations are necessary but you do need to understand what the difference between the two sets of figures or results might mean to the business.

Work systematically and make sure that you comment on each of the seven sets of figures and indicate that you understand what they mean.

You should try to sum up what you have discovered by comparing the two sets of figures and suggest how the business is performing as a result of your findings.

Links To find out more about how financial ratios are used to give insights into a business's performance, the formulae used to calculate them and their limitations as a management tool, see the Revision Guide, pages 76–80.

Total for Question 14 = 12 marks

END OF EXAM

TOTAL FOR SECTION B = 64 MARKS
TOTAL MARKS FOR PAPER = 100 MARKS

Revision test 2

This Workbook is designed to revise skills that might be needed in your exam. The details of your actual exam may change from year to year so always make sure you are up to date. Ask your tutor or check the Pearson website for the most up-to-date Sample Assessment Material to get an idea of the structure of your exam and what this requires of you.

Section A: Personal finance

Answer ALL revision questions. Write your answers in the spaces provided.

Read each question carefully before you start to answer it. Try to answer every question. Check your calculations and show the steps you have used. Check your answers at the end.

There are many different financial organisations and institutions. Each of them has a role to play in financial services.

1 Give **two** roles of the Bank of England.

The primary role is to ensure monetary and financial stability.

(i) ....

....

(ii) ....

....

Total for Question 1 = 2 marks

2 Describe the features of a credit union.

These are community-based financial organisations.

....

....

....

....

Total for Question 2 = 2 marks

3 Explain **two** advantages to customers of banks keeping their branches open.

The question asks for two advantages. Each advantage needs to be explained and linked together.

(i) ....

....

(ii) ....

....

Total for Question 3 = 4 marks

Vihaan and Vanya have saved £40 000 as a deposit on their first home. They have a current account at a high street bank, an ISA at a building society and £1000 of premium bonds. They want to take out a mortgage, but are undecided about the type of mortgage they should apply for.

4 Discuss the differences between a fixed rate and a tracker mortgage.

A fixed rate mortgage has the same interest rate throughout the period of the mortgage. It would give them security about the costs of the mortgage. However, there are disadvantages.

....

....

....

....

....

....

....

....

....

....

....

....

Total for Question 4 = 6 marks

Andy already has a mortgage, but he wonders if he could get a better deal with another lender. He is planning to seek the advice of an independent financial adviser (IFA).

5 Assess what an IFA could offer Andy.

Independent financial advisers should be able to offer whole market financial products. They should recommend the one that best suits Andy.

Total for Question 5 = 10 marks

Jenna needs to borrow £300 to cover her bills. She has reached her overdraft limit with her bank and will not receive her salary for another two weeks. She is considering a payday loan.

Jenna has asked you to help her work out how much she will have paid back at the end of each period and advise her which loan to use.

This table gives information on payday loans.

Table 1: Payday loans information

Provider	APR	Monthly repayment	Terms (months)
A	1081%	£148.02	3
B	1286.9%	£101.63	5
C	1217%	£151.78	3
D	1188%	£235.28	2
E	1717%	£161.04	3

6 Evaluate which payday loan would be the most suitable for Jenna.

Work out the total cost for each of the options and show which offers the lowest cost. Note the differences in number of repayments.

Total for Question = 12 marks

END OF SECTION TOTAL FOR SECTION A = 36 MARKS

Section B: Business finance

Answer ALL questions. Write your answers in the spaces provided.

Oak Toys is the market leader in traditional wooden toys. They have enjoyed a speedy growth due to their products being the complete opposite to high-tech games. The range appeals to parents who want their children to play with toys that stimulate their imagination. All the toys are made in the UK.

7 Identify **two** ways that a business such as Oak Toys could generate revenue income.

Sales are the main source of revenue income, but there are other sources.

(i) ....

....

(ii) ....

....

Total for Question 7 = 2 marks

8 Outline the financial advantages to the company if it were to become a limited company and sell shares to investors.

Shares have a value and investors will pay that amount if they think that the business represents a sound investment.

....

....

....

....

Total for Question 8 = 2 marks

Oak Toys tries to control budgets, but often this fails. The marketing budget was £40 000 but 20% overspent. Purchasing was £124 000 but 15% overspent. Sales budget was £490 000 but 20% up. Overheads, employees and other costs were budgeted at £88 000 but were 10% overspent.

9 (a) Calculate the differences between the actual and budgeted figures, as well as the difference between income and expenditure overall.

5 marks

Construct a budget showing the budgeted figures, the actual figures and the difference between the two.

Show your workings.

£ ....

Oak Toys is owned by four partners:

Franco	40%
Tim	20%
Charlene	10%
Sonal	30%

(b) If the total profit were available to distribute to the partners, what is the share of the profit for Sonal?

3 marks

Assume that the total profit can be shared. Sonal should receive 30% of the total profit.

Show your workings.

£ ....

The company has been analysing the production costs of their top-selling Deluxe Block Builder Set. They sell this product for £99.99.

Table 2: Production costs information

Output	Fixed costs (£)	Variable costs (£)	Total costs (£)
0	15 000	0	15 000
500	15 000	15 000	30 000
1000	15 000	28 000	43 000
2000	15 000	52 000	67 000
3000	15 000	74 000	89 000
4000	15 000	93 000	108 000

(c) Calculate the difference in average cost per unit between the lowest level of output and the highest. Show your workings. **3 marks**

At 500 units: $\frac{30\,000}{500} = £60$

Show your workings.

£ ....

(d) What would be the company's total gross profit at the highest level of output? Show your workings.

3 marks

At 500 total revenue:

Total revenue 500 × £99.99 = £49 995

Total cost @ 500 = £30 000

Therefore £49 995 – £30 000 = £19 995

Show your workings.

£ ....

Total for Question 9 = 14 marks

Oak Toys are keen to develop a range of cheaper wooden toys. They have test launched them at several music festivals over the summer.

The table outlines the selling price, costs and units sold:

	Ring	Ball and hoop	Puzzle	Snake
Selling price per unit	£2	£3	£2.50	£3.50
Labour costs	40p	45p	40p	40p
Material costs	20p	55p	30p	50p
Units sold	9000	12000	6000	4000

10 (a) Which product line provides the best contribution? **8 marks**

For the ring product:

£2 – 60p = £1.40

£1.40 × 9000 = £12 600

Show your workings.

£ ....

(b) If the business has fixed costs of £22 000, what is the level of profit or loss for the business assuming that all four product lines sell the same number of units as in the test period? **2 marks**

Total the contribution of the four product lines and subtract the fixed costs.

Show your workings.

£ ....

Total for Question 10 = 10 marks

The owners of Oak Toys are concerned that sales levels never seem to match production levels. This often means that either they run out of inventory or have too much inventory in the warehouse.

11 Discuss the fact that sales levels are rarely equal to production levels and the implications for break-even calculations.

The break-even point is artificial, so in real life the matched figures are difficult to achieve.

....

....

....

....

....

....

....

....

....

....

....

....

....

....

Total for Question 11 = 6 marks

Oak Toys also sells direct to customers through its website. The owners have prepared their budgeted and actual profit figures for the e-business.

	1st quarter	2nd quarter	3rd quarter	4th quarter
	Budget/Actual	**Budget/Actual**	**Budget/Actual**	**Budget/Actual**
Profit	£5000/(£8000)	£7000/£8000	£9000/£7000	£30 000/£35 000

12 Analyse how the website's yearly profit compares with the budgeted figures. How might the business amend the budget for the next year after seeing these figures?

Budgeted profit was £51 000. Look at the different quarters' results then suggest something in terms of the budgets. Remember that brackets around a figure, e.g. (£8000), indicate a negative figure.

....

....

....

....

....

....

....

....

....

....

....

....

....

....

....

....

Total for Question 12 = 8 marks

13 Assess how the business might have set their budgets, assuming that the first quarter is January, February and March.

Toys are seasonal products, but budgets could also have been based on previous years' sales.

Total for Question 13 = 10 marks

Oak Toys are always looking for ways to improve their profit margins. One of their key sellers is the puzzle pencil case. Normally it sells for £7.99 and the business sells 12 000 of them each year. They want to increase the price to £8.99 but think that sales will fall to 8000.

14 Evaluate the impact the price increase might have on the company's turnover and profits.

12 000 sales @ £7.99 = £95 880
Will 8000 sales @ £8.99 equal this?
What impact will it have on the turnover, profit margin and ability to cover fixed costs?

....

....

....

....

....

....

....

....

....

....

....

....

....

....

....

....

....

....

....

....

....

....

....

Total for Question 14 = 12 marks

END OF EXAM

TOTAL FOR SECTION B = 64 MARKS
TOTAL MARKS FOR PAPER = 100 MARKS

Unit 6: Principles of Management

Your assessment

Unit 6 will be assessed through a task, which will be set by Pearson. You will need to use your understanding of how the role of management and leadership in the workplace contributes towards business success, and produce a report and presentation slides with speaker notes.

Your Revision Workbook

This Workbook is designed to **revise skills** that might be needed in your assessed task. The details of your actual assessed task may change from year to year so always make sure you are up to date. Ask your tutor or check the **Pearson website** for the most up-to-date **Sample Assessment Material** to get an idea of the structure of your assessed task and what this requires of you.

To support your revision, this Workbook contains revision tasks to help you revise the skills that might be needed in your assessed task. The revision tasks are divided into sections.

1 Revision task brief and making notes

In your Workbook you will use your skills to examine a case study and make related notes. You will then apply your learning and preparation to revision activities (pages 78–111).

2 Revision activities

Your response to the activities will help you to revise:

- Analysis and interpretation of business information and data
- Key principles of management
- Suggested alternative management approaches
- Structure and presentation in relation to:
  - Making recommendations through producing a report (pages 87–93; 105–108)
  - Preparing slides with speaker notes for a presentation that explains issues affecting business performance and making recommendations to improve business performance (pages 94–99; 109–111)

Links To help you revise skills that might be needed in your Unit 6 set task, this Workbook contains two revisions tasks starting on pages 78 and 100. The first is guided and models good techniques, to help you develop your skills. The second gives you the opportunity to apply the skills you have developed. See the introduction on page iii for more information on features included to help you revise.

Revision task 1

To support your revision, the revision task below helps you revise the skills that might be needed in your assessed task. The revision task consists of two activities based on a task brief and case study.

The details of the actual assessed task may change so always make sure you are up to date. Ask your tutor or check the Pearson website for the most up-to-date Sample Assessment Material to get an idea of the structure of your assessed task and what this requires of you.

1 Revision task brief

You are working as an assistant to the Finance Director of Brigstone Kitchens, and you have to prepare papers for her to take to a meeting of the board of directors of the company.

Your manager asked you to familiarise yourself with the below sector and company background information in advance of producing these documents.

Task information

Read through the case study a couple of times to give you a good understanding of the challenges faced by the business and the issues involved. You could underline anything you think is significant or jot down short notes beside the information. This will help to get you started on your analysis of the case study.

At this stage, don't be tempted to guess the activities you'll need to complete. Your aim is to prepare for the task through familiarising yourself with the case study.

Brigstone Kitchens Ltd case study

Brigstone Kitchens Ltd, a private limited company, manufactures bespoke fitted kitchen units which are purchased by house builders. The company specialises in the production of traditional handmade units based on kitchen designs provided by builders working on behalf of individual clients. The company prides itself on the quality of its products which use the highest quality materials including expensive wooden cabinet doors and granite worktops rather than the less expensive, ready-to-fit kitchens sold by high street DIY chains.

The company is owned by Carole Saunders who started the business over 30 years ago. From the beginning, in her role as Managing Director, Carole has been actively involved in the management of the company. She is now considering retiring from her day-to-day operational role and wishes to hand over responsibilities to her two children, Peter and Sally.

Peter Saunders, aged 42, joined the company from school. As part of his training, he completed a day-release craft apprenticeship in woodworking skills at a local college, combining the course with his work in the craft section of the company. Eight years ago he moved out of the craft section into an office-based managerial role where he became responsible for sales and ensuring the company complies with health and safety and employment legislation. He has been particularly successful in increasing sales turnover by nearly a quarter of a million pounds over the last five years with turnover increasing from £2 400 000 in 2012 to £2 644 200 in 2016, resulting in an increase in gross profits from £1 400 000 to £1 489 200 over the same period. Peter has a good relationship with the staff who see him as someone who is appreciative of their skills and their commitment to the company.

Sally Evans, aged 38, is the Director of Finance and has been with the company for two years, having previously worked with an international accountancy firm in the City of London for ten years. Since taking up her role she has introduced a new software accounting system, reorganised the duties in the finance section, produced new job descriptions and, upon the retirement of the company's long-serving bookkeeper, created a new job role of Business Support Service Manager, a position that has recently been filled by a business studies graduate from the local university. As part of the changes she is now putting forward, the Business Support Services Manager would be in charge of a newly created Division of Business Support Services which would include the current sales and marketing staff.

The workforce comprises 42 employees. A number of employees have been with the company for over a decade. Carole Saunders has developed a good working relationship with the longer-serving employees who respect her achievement in building up the business and recognise that she is a firm but fair boss who knows her own mind. Carole has always taken a hands-on approach to management and, although there is no up-to-date organisation chart, it is generally accepted by the workforce that the longest-serving employees in each section are responsible for dealing with any day-to-day issues which may arise.

With her finance background Sally has undertaken a review of the company and has concluded that it should formulate a business strategy centred upon the following strategic priorities:

- Growth
- Efficiency savings
- Increases in productivity
- The introduction of new products
- Introducing direct sales to the public

Sally's view is that the first stage in the roll-out of this strategy should be the introduction of a new wage scheme which would link future increases in employees' pay to a performance appraisal system. The proposed new wage scheme will be part of a developing business strategy that will link business objectives to individual performance targets thereby contributing to improvements in business performance.

The proposals to revise the existing performance appraisal system recognise the importance of staff training in upskilling the workforce. Under the new system, managers will be responsible for including an annual staff training target when conducting appraisals with individual staff.

The company's current wage structure and any subsequent wage rises have always been determined by Peter in consultation with his mother, and Sally's proposal to introduce a new wage scheme has resulted in a deterioration in a good working relationship between managers and the workforce.

Although Sally has yet to finalise details of the new wage scheme, a letter signed by the majority of the employees has been sent to Carole Saunders calling for the new scheme to be withdrawn. The letter argues that Brigstone Kitchens Ltd is a profitable company with a track record of continuous growth in sales turnover. Sally, on the other hand, is of the view that the business should use some of its cash reserves, coupled with additional business finance, to establish a new division within the company equipped with new hi-tech machinery which could produce high quality mass-produced kitchen units that would then allow the company to start selling their products directly to the general public. This would result in two new divisions being created, Production and Direct Sales. However, Sally is concerned that it will be difficult to attract potential investors unless management is seen to be tackling some of the company's current issues.

The uncertainty surrounding these proposals is impacting on staff motivation and Carole Saunders has asked Peter and Sally to attend a meeting to discuss the matter in more detail.

In preparation for the meeting Sally has produced the following data sets which have been distributed in advance of the meeting to Carole and Peter.

Table 1: Brigstone Kitchens Ltd – current workforce profile

	Craft section	Assembly section	Finishing section	Finance	Sales	Design
No. of employees	11	12	10	2	3	4
Gender	9 males 2 females	8 males 4 females	7 males 3 females	1 male 1 female	1 males 2 females	2 males 2 females
Average length of service	17 years	12 years	11 years	2 years	3 years	3 years
Average age	57 years	53 years	51 years	25 years	24 years	27 years

Table 2: Brigstone Kitchens Ltd – financial data

	2012	2013	2014	2015	2016
Sales turnover	£2 400 000	£2 509 500	£2 520 000	£2 585 000	£2 644 200
Gross profit	£1 400 000	£1 459 500	£1 460 000	£1 485 000	£1 489 200
Net profit	£440 500	£434 500	£400 750	£389 000	£311 300

Table 3: Brigstone Kitchens Ltd – production data

	2012	2013	2014	2015	2016
Total number of employees	39	40	41	42	42
Average salary	£18 500	£19 000	£19 250	19 500	£20 000
Employees engaged in craft/assembly/finishing sections	30	31	31	32	32
Total units produced per year	12 000	11 950	12 000	11 750	11 700

Don't simply extract figures directly from the table. You need to *analyse* the data – for example in Table 1 you could calculate the percentage of males and females; in Table 2 you could calculate gross and net profit margins; and in Table 3 you could calculate productivity. Also look for trends or relationships between the data sets.

Preparing for your task

Don't be tempted to think of your preparation as the 'answers' to the activities in the revision task. View it instead as a 'tool' for identifying the key management principles you will have studied during your course. You will then be able to identify any gaps in your knowledge prior to completing the task.

It's a good idea to structure your preparation with a focus on different aspects of the case study. This will help you to relate your preparation and learning to the activities later on. The example learner notes below are structured around three main aspects:

1. Key business information and management themes
2. Management issues and principles arising from the case study
3. Possible management strategies to deal with the current issues.

Guided

1. Key business information and management themes

Start with the business information and key management themes since this is where you will be able to identify the main issues and challenges in the case study. These management themes will be related to the topics you have studied during your course – for example, change management, motivation, quality and human resource issues.

- Brigstone Kitchens Ltd – traditional handmade kitchen units
- skilled workers; owner (Carole Saunders) – handing over to two children (Peter and Sally); seems little in the way of a formal management structure (no organisation chart – job descriptions?); business focused upon Carole Saunders
- workers 'contented' but unambitious; workers have been with the company for a long time; probably won't like too much change.

Note how there are already some management themes emerging: no organisation chart or job descriptions; unambitious workers who may not like change. Think of the management principles which you have studied and ask yourself some of the challenges which these may present to management in this case study:

- What are the implications of there being no organisation chart? (Who do the workers report to? Who monitors their work? How are communications between managers and the workforce managed? Who sets the targets?)
- Are there any issues relating to motivation? ('Contented workers' may not necessarily be 'motivated workers'.)
- Why may it be difficult to implement change in the business? (Low labour turnover; workers may not see any reason why the company needs to change.)
- What sort of leadership qualities will be required to implement change in this business? (Inspirational? Energising? An influencer?)
- What management functions will need to come to the fore in order to implement the required changes? (Planning? Organising? Coordinating?)

- Carole: started the business 30 years ago; hands-on
- Peter: knows the company well; considers himself successful (sales figures, gross profit); good relationship with employees; came up from the shop floor; 'craft trained' rather than 'management trained'; understands the nature of the work on the shop floor as well as the business
- Sally: professional accountant; with the company for two years; already reorganised the finance section; wants to implement change across the company as part of a new business strategy; note the strategic priorities she is supporting (growth, efficiency savings, increased productivity, investment etc.)

Managers in a business will have different responsibilities but may also exhibit different styles of management based upon their experience and personal qualities. If the case study refers to different managers try to identify if there are potential issues which may arise when addressing a particular management challenge. Are there any particular issues you could identify which may arise between Carole, Peter and Sally? Will Carole be willing to 'let go of the reins'? How will Peter feel about Sally's wish to implement change in the business? Peter may regard change in exactly the same way as the workforce – could he become as much part of the resistance to change as the workforce? You'll need to think of the management strategies Sally will need to employ in order to support her case for change and how she can persuade Peter to accept that change is necessary.

- Data analysis of company performance – issues re. performance
- Worrying trends in profitability and productivity.

One of the most important aspects of a manager's role is the ability to analyse and interpret data. Having a clear understanding of data will help a manager put together a logically consistent argument to support their case. Look for any trends or relationships in the data set before you undertake any in-depth analysis. You may find it useful to highlight or circle some of the key variables in the data set which identify these trends and relationships. Using arrows is a good way of doing this, for example, in this case study you could identify the increase in gross profit over the five-year period with an arrow pointing upwards ↑ and the decrease in net profit over the period with an arrow pointing downwards↓. These pointers will then be useful when you start to analyse the data in more detail.

2. Management issues and principles arising from the case study

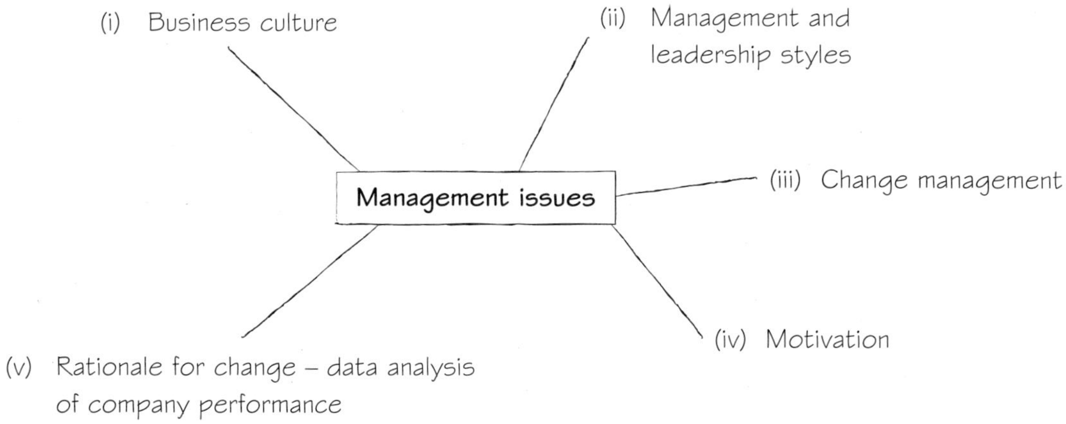

Once you have identified the main management themes it's a good idea to capture them into a set of management issues. This is what effective mangers will do when dealing with a particular management problem. By doing so they are then able to start thinking of their long-term aims and the actions they need to implement in order to secure these aims. Think of it as a series of stages:

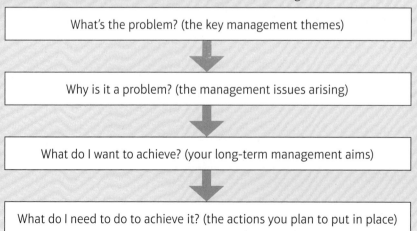

What's the problem? (the key management themes)

↓

Why is it a problem? (the management issues arising)

↓

What do I want to achieve? (your long-term management aims)

↓

What do I need to do to achieve it? (the actions you plan to put in place)

> Remember to look at how management principles can be applied to the case study. Identifying these management principles will then enable you to undertake follow-up reading of your course work notes to make sure you fully understand how these management principles can be applied to the case study.

(i) Business culture

- 'How things are done around here'; impact of any changes on business culture (Sally's new strategy on the company's vision and mission – does it have a mission and vision?)
- Need to introduce more formalised policies and procedures – impact on employees (opposition? how to achieve employee buy-in?)

> Continue to identify the questions and challenges which need to be addressed in relation to each of the management principles you have identified.

(ii) Management and leadership styles

Types of leadership styles: autocratic, democratic, paternalistic, laissez faire, transactional, transformational, charismatic

- Carole Saunders (owner): elements of inspiring/charismatic/autocratic ('knows her own mind'?)
- Peter: paternalistic, laissez faire (no organisation chart; the longest-serving employees in each section are responsible for dealing with any day-to-day issues which may arise); no formal business qualifications
- Sally: transformational? (accounting background; already reorganised the finance section; new post created; taking charge of a company review – new strategic objectives formulated), proposing a significant change in the company's strategic objectives, e.g. new products and selling directly to the public – backed by external finance from new investors/financial institutions

> Note how section (ii) refers to specialist management terms – paternalistic, transformational, laissez faire. You may need to remind yourself of what these terms mean by referring to your course work notes. You can then add a short note to remind yourself of the characteristics of each type of management and leadership style.

(iii) Change management

The need to manage change for business survival and growth.

Identifying the need for change:

- Impact on employees: change in working practices; resistance to change; what are their fears (less pay? May have to work harder to achieve an increase in pay? Who will set the targets? Will the targets be too difficult to achieve?); age profile of current workforce could also be an issue (particularly in the 'production' sections of the company) – may be more difficult for them to embrace change; may result in a change in business culture.
- Impact on Carole and Peter: new approach to management; more direction provided to the workforce (setting targets); management by objectives (setting SMART targets, monitoring); less laissez–faire approach to management; Peter may feel threatened by Sally and may lack confidence in his managerial ability to implement the changes (even if he can be convinced to support them); Sally has already started the process of change in the Finance section; Peter may also be concerned that he will no longer have the day-to-day support of the owner of the business.
- Impact on management systems: introduction of performance appraisal (purpose of performance appraisal – targets, performance, provide feedback, identify training needs); organisation chart, job descriptions and new job roles (supervisory function to be introduced?); training and development.

(iv) Motivation

Impact of motivation in the workplace; strategies for improving motivation (link to motivational theorists – Maslow hierarchy, Herzberg – hygiene and motivation factors, Mayo – team work); examples of financial and non-financial motivators

(v) Rationale for change

Data analysis of company performance – key points and implications:

You may need to provide evidence in your response to activities that you can analyse and evaluate management information and data. Remember that management information is processed data – in other words it is data that has been analysed in such a way as to enable a manager to make decisions or formulate a strategy. By this stage you will have already identified some trends (look at the arrows you have already pencilled into the data set). You now need to analyse the implications of these trends for the business.

- Table 1: average age in the production section is high, particularly in the craft section (57 years; predominantly male); risk factors (approaching retirement/end of working life? potential health issues? productivity issues?); will the company be able to recruit suitably qualified and experienced craft employees in the future?; business support staff are younger and could be more willing to take on new job roles.
- Table 2: sales and gross profit have increased year on year for the last five years (positive point) BUT both gross and net profit margins have FALLEN over the last five years (e.g. 2012: gross profit margin (0.58); net profit margin (0.18); 2016: gross profit margin (0.56); net profit margin (0.12)); the fall in net profit margin is significant with a downward year-on-year trend – possible impact of increased operating expenses – this calls for a systematic review of functions of management, i.e. planning, organising, coordinating, monitoring and delegating.
- Table 3: productivity is falling (ref: in the craft/assembly and finishing sections productivity has fallen from 400 units per worker per year (2012) to 365 units per worker per year (2016)); impact on efficiency and costs?

One of the most compelling arguments for change is to identify if a business is meeting its long-term objectives. For most businesses these objectives will be focused upon profits and productivity or sub-sets of each. For example, poor customer service is a sub-set of profitability because if customers are dissatisfied then they will switch to other businesses. Similarly, motivation and costs are sub-sets of productivity since poor motivation will impact directly on the amount produced per employee and low levels of productivity will impact upon labour costs.

Your data analysis should therefore involve some calculations. Calculating percentages and ratios are useful ways to exemplify a certain point. For example, in these notes the analysis of Table 2 includes both aggregate figures (for gross and net profits) as well as ratio analysis (to determine gross and net profit margins).

Undertaking this level of analysis would enable you to put together a rationale for a proposed management strategy and related management actions.

You might find it useful to follow these stages when you analyse the data:

- Identify high-level trends (use the arrows).
- Work out high-level changes in the variables – by how much has one of the variables increased or decreased?
- Use the outcomes in the section on key business information and management themes (page 81) to identify the percentage change in the variables. You could also undertake some ratio analysis at this stage.
- Start to draw some conclusions from your analysis. Are there any presenting issues? In this case study, for example, both gross and net profits have increased for the last five years, but gross and net profit margins have fallen.
- How will these conclusions influence your management strategy?
- It's also useful to identify the implications for the business if it doesn't address the issues you have identified in the analysis of the data.

3. Possible management strategies to deal with the current issues

- Establish a clear vision and rationale for change: stress the urgency of the change (performance).
- Engage with employees – call a meeting/work with individuals (influencers/leaders).
- Identify win–win scenarios for managers and employees.
- Publish an up-to-date organisation chart.
- Create winners in the workforce.
- Implement new policies and procedures.
- Communicate and celebrate gains (confirm the vision).
- Embed the procedures into the 'fabric' of company management.
- Establish a training programme including new induction programme.
- Monitor results.
- Continue to celebrate achievements – communicate and receive feedback from employees.

This looks straightforward but management is never that easy – look at the fifth bullet point: 'Create winners in the workforce'. It's easy to deal with winners. They'll be motivated, may have been promoted or even have had an increase in pay. But for every winner there may be a loser, or worse still, maybe even more than one loser – those individuals in the workforce who miss out on promotion or who don't get an increase in pay. What will be your management strategy for dealing with these people? What management principles will you apply? What functions of management and leadership will you need to call upon?

Once you have considered the different aspects of the case study put down some thoughts about how you would deal with the issues you have identified. Don't think of this as the *correct answer* to any activity in the revision task. One way of approaching this is to think of how you would respond if you were part of a group of management learners discussing the case study and were asked your views of what you would do.

Links To find out more about individual management issues, see the Revision Guide:

- Business culture, page 94
- Leadership styles, page 95
- Managing change, page 112
- Motivating employees, pages 104–106
- Analysing data, page 120.

Complete some revision activities of your own as part of your preparation for the revision task. Try these activities in relation to the Brigstone Kitchens Ltd case study. You may need to use additional paper in addition to the space here.

1. Describe how would you motivate the workers to accept any changes.

2. Formulate an argument you could put forward to Peter regarding the performance of the company which would convince him of the need for change.

3. Construct a new organisation chart for the company. Suggest some titles for the new positions in the company.

2 Revision activities

You must complete ALL activities.

> To answer the two revision questions you will have read a case study (pages 79–80) and carried out related preparation (pages 81–86). In your actual assessment you may not be allowed to use your preparatory notes, or there may be restrictions on the length and type of notes that are allowed. The case study will be provided with the activities, for your reference. Check with your tutor or look at the latest Sample Assessment Material on the Pearson website for details.

Your activities will result in two outcomes:

- A report
- Presentation slides with speaker notes

Revision activity 1

> For Revision activity 1, you are asked to prepare a formal report. You should check with your tutor or look at the latest Sample Assessment Material on the Pearson website for details of what is required in your actual assessment.

With reference to the information on Brigstone Kitchens Ltd, you have been asked to prepare a report for the Finance Director analysing the current challenges faced by the company and proposing the management actions that could be implemented to address these challenges.

Use the space below to write your formal report. You could word process it if you prefer.

> When responding to an activity that requires you to propose a set of management actions, there is likely to be no single 'correct answer'. The key is to think about the business's priorities in order to identify issues which may impact negatively on its ability to achieve its business objectives. You will then need to base your suggested management actions on addressing these issues and challenges.
>
> From your earlier analysis of the case study, you should have identified Sally's proposals for the company's strategic priorities.

> You have been asked to write a formal report, so you should start with the conventional headings used in business reports.

Guided

Formal report on the current management challenges facing Brigstone Kitchens and suggested management actions

This report has been compiled by .... and is intended for the Finance Director

Recommendations for discussion

Date: ....

> Start the report with a short introduction in which you clearly identify the structure of what each section of the report will cover.

1. Introduction

1.1 The purpose of this report is to:

(i) propose a set of new strategic priorities

(ii) analyse the impact of the current management challenges faced by Brigstone Kitchens Ltd

(iii) ....

(iv) ....

It's a good idea to write stand-alone sections which follow the points you have raised in the Introduction. Each section should be numbered with a heading (use bold font in a word-processed document); focus on the main issues and number each sub-point. This makes it easier for participants at the meeting to refer easily to the specific points you are raising.

In this case study the individual sections of the report could relate to:

(i) the strategic priorities put forward by Sally, the Finance Director

(ii) the current challenges facing the business

(iii) the impact of these challenges on the business

(iv) your recommendations for addressing the challenges.

It would also be acceptable to combine together section (ii) the current challenges facing the business with section (iii) the impact of these challenges on the business to create one section with the title *'The impact of the current challenges facing the business'*. The main point to remember is that there is likely to be no *one correct answer* and that it is important to consider:

- the format and layout of your report, i.e. does the report follow normal business conventions?
- the content of your report, i.e. the use of appropriate business terminology
- the logical sequencing of your report, i.e. does one section naturally follow on to the next section?
- the quality of your data analysis
- your ability to show how the principles of management can be applied in a practical business setting
- the quality of your recommendations. Are they practical and cost effective? Will they address the challenges you have identified? Have you considered the impact on the business if your recommendations are not approved?

Note how the first section of the report has been structured. It has a heading which is numbered and then separate sub-sections which follow sequentially.

2. Proposed key strategic objectives

2.1 The business is currently facing significant changes to its management team with both the Director of Operations and the Director of Finance likely to take on additional management responsibilities when the owner of the company relinquishes her current operational management duties.

2.2 This significant change in management responsibilities presents the company with the opportunity to establish a set of new strategic objectives which will prepare the company for the next stage in its development.

What do you consider to be the five main areas that the business should consider changing to improve its performance?

2.3 The proposed strategic priorities are as follows:

....

....

....

....

....

....

....

2.4 ....

....

....

....

....

....

....

....

Keep the report formal – don't include first names. Sally, for example, should be referred to as the Director of Finance throughout the report.

Don't write in the first person i.e. *'I think it's a good idea if we …'.* Instead write *'The following proposals are presented for consideration by management …'.*

Section 3 of the report looks at the current management challenges faced by Brigstone Kitchens Ltd. Refer to the case study for the details of the data.

3. Current management challenges faced by Brigstone Kitchens Ltd

3.1 looks at the data analysis. Notice how each sub-section *starts with the analysis* and then *draws a conclusion* or considers the implications for the business. In (ii) you will need to write a section on your analysis of profitability. The following stages may help you:

(a) Start by identifying what has happened to sales turnover over a five-year period and the impact on gross profit (provide the figures and remember how percentages can be used as a way of focusing on, or emphasising, a particular trend).

(b) Add a note of caution by referring to the trend in gross and net profit margins (provide the figures).

(c) Finish off with the implications for the company and hint at what may need to be done in order to address the issue that you have identified.

3.1 An analysis of the three data tables that accompany this report highlight a number of challenges which must be addressed by management:

(i) The current profile of the total workforce (Table 1) shows that it is predominantly male (66%) with this figure increasing to 77.7% in the combined craft, assembly and finishing sections. The age profile in these three sections is 50 years or above with the average age in the craft section rising to 57 years. The challenges which must be addressed by management focus upon the future recruitment of highly skilled craft workers, the upskilling of the current workforce, motivation and the willingness or otherwise of the workforce to accept changes in business practices.

Refer back to the previous hint box for guidance on how to approach parts (ii) and (iii).

(ii) ....

....

....

....

....

....

....

(iii) ....

....

It's also acceptable to use charts and diagrams since they are useful visual aids for getting across a particular point.

The remaining sections in Part 3 of the report consider the other management challenges faced by Brigstone Kitchens Ltd – management style (3.2), business culture (3.3), business structure (3.4) and motivation (3.5). Again note how each of these separate sections follows a similar structure:
- Identification of the issue
- Impact on the business
- Possible solution to address the issue identified

3.2 The management style adopted by the company's management team has resulted in low staff turnover. Employees respect the owner of the company, have significant autonomy in operational matters and are self-managed. There are few policies and procedures which results in a 'can do' attitude. These elements of a laissez-faire approach to management can bring significant benefits but can also result in difficulties, particularly if things start to go wrong since the levels of responsibility and accountability may be difficult to identify without a formal organisation chart and reporting structure.

3.3 The prevailing business culture – 'how things are done around here' – means that it is difficult to implement any significant changes to organisational practices apart from in specific sections of the workforce when personnel changes occur resulting in the recruitment of new employees. For example, in the Finance Section, a new Business Support Manager has been appointed which, along with the installation of the new accounting software, will make it easier to set and monitor budgets and identify potential efficiency savings.

Complete section 3.3 by identifying the potential issues that can be associated with the prevailing business culture. Why might the culture within this organisation be a problem? Can you see any examples in the case study that suggest there is an existing problem?

....

3.4 The lack of an identified management hierarchy and structure in the form of an organisation chart means that introducing policies and procedures for the management of physical and human resources is an additional challenge.

Complete Section 3.4 by discussing the impact of the lack of an organisation chart and a formalised management hierarchy on the business. You should consider such aspects as policies and procedures and setting and monitoring business targets and objectives and why these are important.

3.5 There is also an issue of employee motivation in the company.

Using your knowledge of report writing and referring to the approach you have taken with the other parts of this section complete 3.5. Think about the benefits of a motivated workforce and the impact of a workforce who will not accept change. Are there any motivational theories you can refer to which will back up your arguments?

By this stage in your report you will have covered the management issues and challenges and the impact on business performance. The final part of your report should cover the proposals you wish the company to support. A good way of doing this is to have two separate sections – one which proposes the specific management actions to address the management challenge and then a set of recommendations which form the management strategy for implementing these actions.

Section 4 is based upon a range of actions which could be adopted by the company. They should be practical and realistic and provide the basis for moving forward.

4. Proposals to address the current management issues

4.1 Establish a clear vision for the company, agreed by senior managers who will be responsible for communicating this vision to the workforce.

4.2 Engage in on-going discussions with the workforce to stress the urgency of the need for change centred upon the company's five-year trends in performance.

4.3 Produce a new draft organisation chart which introduces the role of Section Supervisor. As the first stage in this process, the Business Support Services Manager would take on line management responsibility for a newly created Division of Business Support Services which will integrate the staff currently working in finance, sales and design. In addition two new divisions will be created – Production and Direct Sales.

Now complete the remaining proposals – you may think that there are more than seven things that need to be done – but don't make the list so long that it becomes unmanageable. The other proposals could be drawn from the management actions identified in your preparation or you may have since thought about others which are more relevant.

The actions should relate to the challenges identified in Section 3 of the report – culture, motivation, target-setting, policies and procedures, training and skills.

Remember too that both the owner (Carole) and the current Director of Operations (Peter) may lack experience of managing strategic change so they may need some help in this aspect of management.

4.4 ....

....

....

....

4.5 ....

....

4.6 ....

....

....

4.7 ....

....

....

Section 5 follows on logically and answers the question *'If we want to implement all of these actions what do we need to put in place which will enable us to do so and who needs to be responsible for taking forward the actions?'* In other words, who will do what?

This final section of the report contains the recommendations you are putting forward. In this case the report suggests a Management Implementation Plan – in other words how the proposed actions could be implemented. Think of the implementation plan as a management framework in which management responsibilities are clearly allocated. They must therefore be allocated in such a way as to take account of the responsibilities, skills and experience of managers in the team. In this case there is the owner and two senior managers – the Director of Finance and the Director of Operations.

5. Recommendations

5.1 It is recommended that a Management Implementation Plan is devised comprising the following elements:

(i) Senior managers agree a new set of strategic objectives based upon the strategic priorities identified in this report.

(ii) The owner takes responsibility for formulating a communications strategy focused upon workforce engagement.

(iii) The owner and senior managers design a new pay scheme based upon performance targets in each of the Divisions and these form the basis of targets for individual employees established within a new performance appraisal scheme.

Think of two further recommendations and who would take responsibility for their implementation.

(iv) ....

....

....

....

....

....

....

(v) ....

....

....

....

....

....

....

Now review your recommendations:

- Have you identified the key challenges and drivers for change?
- Have you analysed the data presented in the case study and drawn the relevant conclusions from your analysis?
- Are your proposals and recommendations *logically consistent, practical and workable*? Do they take account of any budgetary considerations?

You could look back at your preparation on pages 81–84 to help your review.

Revision activity 2

For Revision activity 2, you are asked to prepare a maximum of six presentation slides and accompanying speaker notes. You should check with your tutor or look at the latest Sample Assessment Material on the Pearson website for details of what is required in your actual assessment.

Prepare a maximum of six slides with speaker notes for a presentation to be given by the Finance Director to the board of Brigstone Kitchens, in which you:

- identify the implications of the issues facing the company
- recommend a set of management actions that could be implemented.

Base your presentation slides around the format of your report. Imagine that you have presented the report and that you have prepared these presentation slides so that you can highlight or provide more details on specific aspects of the report.

Pay particular attention to the number of slides you have been asked to prepare – up to a maximum of six slides here.

Guided

Create six boxes to represent each of the slides.

Number each of the slides from 1 to 6.

Give each slide a heading based on the sections in your report.

Note down the points you will include on each slide mapped against your report.

Slide 1, for example, could identify what you are going to cover in your presentation.

When you have prepared each slide check to see that you have covered all the main points.

1. Brigstone Kitchens Ltd
Improving management effectiveness and business performance
- Key strategic priorities
- Challenges
- Performance
- Proposals
- Implementation plan

2. Key strategic priorities
- Growth
- Productivity
- New products
- Direct sales

3. Current management challenges
- Workforce profile
- Management
- Business performance

4. Business performance
[Graph of profitability]

5. Proposals
- Vision
- Communications
- Wage scheme
- Policies and procedures
- Training needs analysis
- Managing strategic change

6. Management implementation plan
- Strategic objectives
- Communications with the workforce
- New pay scheme
- Organisation chart
- Business plan
- Costings

Links Presentations are covered on page 125 of the Revision Guide.

Don't make the slides too 'fussy' – too many images will get in the way of the key messages you are trying to get across to your audience. In order to make your presentation more than just a series of bullet points you can:

- Include a limited number of images which get across the point you are trying to make – an image should 'add value' to the presentation slide.
- Include charts and diagrams.
- Include graphs which clearly show the trends in aspects of business activity such as profits, costs, productivity and sales turnover.

Guided

Slide 1

1. Brigstone Kitchens Ltd

Improving management effectiveness and business performance

- Strategic priorities – identifying the way forward
- Business performance and the need for change
- Current management challenges
- ....
- ....
- ....

Use the first slide to highlight the areas you will cover in your slides. Add any additional bullet points you think will need to be covered.

Slide 1 speaker notes

- Introduce the presentation – context of the introduction of the new pay scheme
- ....
....
- ....
....

Don't write a script – in other words don't write out word for word what you are going to say in your presentation. Your speaker notes are exactly that – **notes** – they should be in a format which you can easily expand on in the presentation. Bullet points are a good way of writing speaker notes.

Slide 2

2. Key strategic priorities

- Growth
- Efficiency savings
- Increased productivity
- Introduction of new products
- Introducing direct sales to the public

Once again, refer to your report to extract the necessary points you want to highlight in your presentation. In Slide 2, for example, you may go through each strategic priority.

Add an image which you think captures the points being made on this slide.

Slide 2 speaker notes

- Growth – new products; new markets; opportunities to improve profitability (gross and net profit margins); attract new investors
- ....
....
- ....
....
- ....
....
- ....
....

You'll only have enough space on the slide to list the strategic priorities, so your speaker notes should be used to provide more details on why these are the Finance Director's strategic priorities – for example, generating efficiency savings would have a direct impact upon net profit margins.

Slide 3

3. Current management challenges

Management challenge	Impact on the business
Workforce profile	Motivation to take on new responsibilities
Management	No defined structure
Business performance	Inefficiencies

Slide 3 speaker notes

- Impact of workforce profile – composition; motivation; recruitment
- ....
  ....
- ....
  ....

You'll now have to start thinking about how to present the management challenges currently facing the company and their influence on company performance.

Most presentational software will allow you to choose the format of individual slides. In this case it would be useful to select a format which allows you to include a table in the slide. You could then use a two-column table in which each management challenge or issue is listed in one column and its impact identified in the second column.

Add to your speaker notes some additional points identifying the impact on the business for each of the three management challenges identified in the table.

Charts, tables and diagrams are a good way of presenting a visual representation of a complex data set. You can do this by entering data into a spreadsheet then converting the data into a chart and inserting the chart directly onto one of the presentation slides.

Slide 4

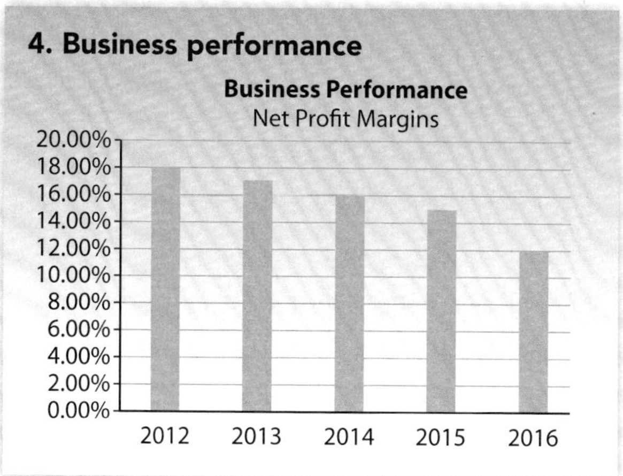

Slide 4 speaker notes

- Increase in sales turnover (positive) – commend Peter's effort
- ....
  ....
- ....
  ....

BUT

- ....
  ....

If the appropriate data set in the case study allows, it is always useful to include a slide which shows trends in business performance because you can use it to support your argument for change. Slide 4 includes a chart which has been imported from a spreadsheet.

Use a spreadsheet to prepare a chart on another aspect of the company's performance to replace the current chart which appears on Slide 4.

When presenting a chart, for example, point out any trends, the impact of these trends and compare them with other variables in the data set from which they are drawn. For example in this case study, both sales turnover and gross profits are increasing year-on-year but net profit margins are falling. Can you think of any other factors which have impacted on the trend in performance shown in your graph?

Slide 5

5. Management proposals

Proposal	Rationale
Agree strategic objectives	To determine the long-term direction of the business
Communication strategy	To share the vision with the workforce
New organisation chart	To create the new departments
New wage scheme	
Update policies and procedures	

Slide 5 could identify specific proposals which could be introduced by the company. You should have listed some of these in your preparation, and your report will have provided further details on your proposals. Tables are a good way of getting across action plans because you can identify the action in one column and the reason or rationale for the action in another column.

Slide 5 speaker notes

- Agree strategic objectives: strategy is concerned with the long term; stress the urgency of the change (performance); identify the risks if the company doesn't change
- Need for a clear business plan if we need to raise additional capital to finance the proposed new developments
- ....
  ....
- ....
  ....
- ....
  ....
- ....
  ....
- ....
  ....
- ....
  ....

PLUS

- ....
  ....

Your speaker notes should provide a few pointers regarding how each of the proposals will address the current challenges faced by the company.

Insert the rationale for the remaining two proposals in Slide 5.

Slide 6

Your final slide should summarise the implications of the main points in your presentation leading to a set of recommendations. There a number of ways that this could be presented:

- A series of bullet points
- A table
- A chart
- An organisation chart.

6. Recommendations

WHAT?	WHY?	WHO?
Agree strategic objectives	To establish long-term vision	Owner plus senior managers
Communications with the workforce	To establish 'workforce buy-in'	Owner
New pay scheme		
Organisation chart		
Business plan		
Costings		

The heading and the first two recommendations have been completed for you. Add to the electronic version of your slide any other recommendations which you want to put forward.

Slide 6 speaker notes

- Proposed strategic priorities → management challenges and impact → actions → recommendations
- ....
- ....

....

....

....

....

In this case study the recommendations revolve around the management of change. You've already covered the reasons for the changes required, so now your audience will want to know your recommendations for taking forward your proposals.

Slide 6 summarises the presentation by focusing on *what* needs to be done, *why* it needs to be done and *who* will take the management lead in ensuring that it is implemented.

A good way of finishing a presentation is to:

(i) Provide a very brief overview of what you have tried to show in the presentation.

(ii) Ask if the audience has any questions.

(iii) Finish with your own question.

(iv) Remember to thank the audience for their attention.

Revision task 2

To support your revision, the revision task below helps you revise the skills that might be needed in your assessed task. The revision task consists of two activities based on a task brief and case study.

The details of the actual assessed task may change so always make sure you are up to date. Ask your tutor or check the Pearson website for the most up-to-date Sample Assessment Material to get an idea of the structure of your assessed task and what this requires of you.

1 Revision task brief

You are working as an assistant to the Managing Director of The Brompton Group plc and you have to prepare papers for the Managing Director to take to the Board of Directors.

Your manager asked you to familiarise yourself with the below sector and company background information in advance of producing these documents.

For this activity you will need to carry out your own preparation.

Read the case study carefully to give you a good understanding of the challenges faced by the business and the issues involved. You could underline anything you think is significant or jot down short notes beside the information. This will help you in identifying the managerial issues and the business principles that you might recommend to resolve them. Analyse the data in the case study and draw some conclusions.

Task information

The Brompton Group plc case study

The Brompton Group plc is a well-established company and in 2015 employed a workforce of 14 000 employees, which increased to 18 500 in 2016. The company specialises in two main areas – the International Transport Group focuses on the design, manufacture and distribution of parts for high-speed rail systems and underground rail networks in the UK and in the European Union and the Automotive Group supplies spare parts for motor cars to high street retailers and garages. The company is located in the south-east of England and has two regional warehouse distribution facilities in the Midlands and the north-east of England. The company's organisational structure comprises the following divisions – Production (UK Division), Production (International Division), Product Design and Research (Rail), Motor Parts (Retail), Motor Parts (Business), Sales and Marketing, Finance, Human Resources, Training and Development, Quality Assurance, Customer Services, Warehouse and Distribution, Online Sales (motor parts), Administration and IT services. Each division has a director and, at an operational level, supervisors have line management responsibility. Some divisions also have team leaders who report directly to supervisors.

The Brompton Group plc is having to address a number of challenges. Competition from emerging economies in the Far East has resulted in an increase in low-cost imported spare parts for motor cars, the company is finding it difficult to recruit suitably qualified employees, particularly engineers, and there have been significant technical issues with the recently introduced online sales platform which have resulted in an increase in the number of customer complaints. The impact on the company of the UK's decision to leave the European Union has created uncertainty regarding the company's long-term investment strategy.

The company's new Managing Director (MD) has been given the responsibility for undertaking a management review aimed at addressing these issues. The MD has determined that the first stage of the management review will consider three main areas. The background to these three main areas is provided in the following sections.

1. Company performance

The company's income statement for the last two years is shown below:

Income Statement for the year ended 31 March 2016

	2015 £m	2016 £m
Revenue	2300	2700
Cost of sales	1745	2272
Gross profit	555	428
Operating expenses	252	362
Operating profit	303	66
Interest payable	18	32
Profit before taxation	285	34
Taxation	60	4
Profit for the year	225	30*

* The company's share price on 31 March 2016 was £2.47 compared with £4.65 on 31 March 2015. The corresponding figures for the FTSE 100 were 6125 (31 March 2015) and 5975 (31 March 2016).

2. Restructuring of the company

The MD considers that the current structure of the company is not fit for purpose and that a reorganisation of the company would result in a more efficient and streamlined management structure. The MD's plan is to restructure the business in such a way that it can meet the current challenges it faces. The restructuring will result in a revised organisation chart.

The MD is also concerned that some senior managers are doing too much routine work themselves rather than managing their time to focus upon their key management functions.

The managers, on the other hand, consider that many of the current supervisors in the company do not possess the necessary skills to enable the managers to delegate tasks to them. In addition managers fear that by delegating tasks to the supervisors they will lose control of operational issues which will impact negatively upon their ability to achieve their own annual performance targets and, as a result, they will lose out financially since these targets form part of the manager's remuneration package.

Supervisors are not keen to take on more delegated tasks since this will give them more responsibility to deal with day-to-day operational issues such as work rotas, customer service issues and scheduling of work to meet production targets.

Soundings from the workforce consider that the Managing Director's proposal to review the company's management structure is the first stage in reducing the overall size of the workforce in order to implement cost-cutting measures.

3. Quality assurance

The company's current quality assurance system is based upon two main aspects:

- Quality control inspections in the Production Divisions
- Analysing the responses to customer questionnaires using the online sales platform.

The MD wishes to implement a recognised accredited quality system which covers all aspects of company management systems and processes; however, the MD has yet to determine which quality system will best serve the needs of the company.

Preparing for your task

When preparing for the revision task look for 'pointers' which link in to your knowledge of the 'principles of management'. This will then enable you to focus your background research on specific aspects of the Unit. In this case study these principles centre upon aspects such as managing change, quality management, business culture and the structure of the workforce. Prior to completing the activities you should have read up on all of these aspects.

Use the space below and any additional paper you need to complete your preparation and notes. You could word-process your notes if you prefer.

From the case study material you are already aware that the Managing Director wants to restructure the company. Look at different models of how this could be done and prepare two or three different organisation charts so that you can review the options available. Remember, there are no 'correct answers' (although it would not be a good idea to put together divisions which are too diverse, for example merging Human Resources with Warehouse and Distribution). You should aim for something that is logically consistent and would be able to take forward the company's strategic objectives.

Links To find out more about individual management issues, see the Revision Guide:

- Business culture, page 94
- Managing change, page 112
- Quality management, page 116
- Structure of the workforce, pages 94 and 101.

2 Revision activities

You must complete ALL activities.

To answer the two revision questions you will have read a case study (pages 101-102) and carried out related preparation (pages 103–104). In your actual assessment you may not be allowed to use your preparatory notes, or there may be restrictions on the length and type of notes that are allowed. The case study will be provided with the activities, for your reference. Check with your tutor or look at the latest Sample Assessment Material on the Pearson website for details.

Your activities will result in two outcomes:

- A report
- Presentation slides with speaker notes

Revision activity 1

For Revision activity 1, you are asked to prepare a formal report. You should check with your tutor or look at the latest Sample Assessment Material on the Pearson website for details of what is required in your actual assessment.

With reference to information provided on The Brompton Group plc in the case study, you are an assistant in a business advisory service and have been asked to prepare a report for your manager, including a set of recommendations that could address the priorities identified by the Managing Director.

Use the space below to write your formal report. You could word-process it if you prefer.

Remember the good practice points when writing a formal business report – title of the report, who wrote the report, who it is for and the date the report was presented. Remember to start with an introduction and then write separate numbered points which cover the points you have highlighted in the introduction to the report.

Plan out your report so that it logically follows an argument, rationale or set of recommendations. You could start with an introduction, then follow on with an analysis of company performance which would then lead on to two sections, one looking at restructuring and a second looking at quality.

When presenting your recommendations consider:

1. if some have a higher priority than others – if so, put these first
2. if some recommendations rely on other actions before they can be implemented – if so, put your recommendations in a logical sequence.

The rationale for any change must be based on an analysis of performance.

If performance is poor, why is it poor and what can be done to make it better? If performance is good, why is it good and how can this performance be sustained and improved upon?

You should have already analysed the performance of The Brompton Group plc in your preparation. Use the income statement to do this – look for potential problems (profits are a good place to start); can you identify any factors in the case study which may have impacted upon profit levels? What is the relationship between profits and share prices? What is the potential impact of fluctuations in share prices on the company? What relevance is the FTSE 100 when evaluating the performance of the company's share price (in this case both the FTSE 100 and the company's share prices have both gone down)?

Managers are sometimes called upon to make difficult decisions and all decisions have consequences – sometimes good, sometimes not so good – particularly for the people affected by those decisions. Restructuring management responsibilities is a case in point – there are likely to be winners and losers. Think about how you are going to manage the losers. Are there any constraints which may limit the things you can do?

Revision activity 2

For Revision activity 2, you are asked to prepare a maximum of six presentation slides and accompanying speaker notes. You should check with your tutor or look at the latest Sample Assessment Material on the Pearson website for details of what is required in your actual assessment.

Prepare a maximum of six slides with speaker notes for a presentation to be given by the Managing Director to the board of The Brompton Group, in which you:

- analyse the rationale for change in The Brompton Group plc
- recommend a set of proposed management actions.

You can write your slides and speaker notes here, or alternatively just use these spaces for brief planning. You may prefer to prepare your slides and speaker notes using presentation software on a computer.

Slide 1

1 ....

....

....

....

....

....

....

The slide presentation should follow the sequence of your business report. So look at the introduction to your report as the basis for preparing Slide 1. Make sure that all your slides have a heading.

Slide 1 speaker notes

....

....

....

....

....

....

....

....

....

....

Slide 2

2 ....

....

....

....

....

....

....

If the second section in your report is an analysis of business performance then Slide 2 could summarise your findings either in a bullet point format or using charts and diagrams – graphs are always useful because they can show trends in a visual format. You will need to create a spreadsheet of the data and then insert the graph into the slide presentation. All graphs should have a title and be clearly labelled.

Slide 2 speaker notes

....

....

....

....

....

....

....

....

....

....

Slide 3

3 ....

....

....

....

....

....

Don't include lots of detail in your individual slides. Bullet points, flow charts or diagrams are useful ways of condensing points into two or three key words (e.g. bullet points) or showing relationships and processes (flow charts). Practise using different types of software so that you can cut and paste flow carts and diagrams into your slide presentation.

Slide 3 speaker notes

....

....

....

....

....

....

....

....

....

....

If you are using a flow chart or process cycle your speaker notes should refer to all the elements noted in the diagrams.

Slide 4

4 ....

....

....

....

....

....

....

Computer software packages will allow you to insert organisation charts into your documents which you can then cut and paste into your slide presentation. Practise doing this so that you are confident in using these skills when completing the activity.

Slide 4 speaker notes

....

....

....

....

....

....

....

....

....

....

If you're going to include an organisation chart your speaker notes should refer to:

- the rationale behind the structure – for example, why you have chosen to combine together two functions or divisions
- the benefits which will accrue to the company
- the possible implications of the new structure, e.g. any job losses; timelines for the introduction.

Slide 5

5 ....

....

....

....

....

....

....

Visual representations and images can be a useful way of getting over your points. But don't let them 'take over' from the content of your presentation.

Slide 5 speaker notes

....

....

....

....

....

....

....

....

....

....

Don't try to explain an image to the audience – if you have to explain what the image means it probably means that you've chosen the wrong image. Always include text (bullet points or flow charts) which clearly shows what the image is trying to convey.

Slide 6

6 ....

....

....

....

....

....

....

The final slide should summarise your presentation; in this activity you are required to present your recommendations. Refer back to the recommendations in your report to make sure that you've covered all of them. Number your recommendations and ensure that they logically follow on from the sequence of the slides in your presentation.

Slide 6 speaker notes

....

....

....

....

....

....

....

....

....

....

Although it's good practice to thank your audience, it's not good practice to include the words 'thank you' on your final presentation slide – it wastes valuable space on the slide which you could use for making another point to support your arguments.

Unit 7: Business Decision Making

Your assessment

Unit 7 will be assessed through a task, which will be set by Pearson. You will need to use your skills relating to business concepts, processes and data to enable the formulation of business decisions and solutions. You will demonstrate your ability to extract relevant information from a case study/business scenario and apply the knowledge and understanding you have developed.

Your Revision Workbook

This Workbook is designed to **revise skills** that might be needed in your assessed task. The details of your actual assessed task may change from year to year so always make sure you are up to date. Ask your tutor or check the **Pearson website** for the most up-to-date **Sample Assessment Material** to get an idea of the structure of your assessed task and what this requires of you. Make sure you check the instructions in relation to taking a calculator into the assessed task, and completing the activities using a computer.

To support your revision, this Workbook contains revision tasks to help you revise the skills that might be needed in your assessed task.

Revision task

In your Workbook you will use your skills to:

- Extract relevant information from a case study/business scenario
- Apply the knowledge and understanding you have developed

Your response to the activities will help you to revise:

- Business plans
- Decision making in business
- Use of research to justify the marketing of a business
- Efficient operational management of the business
- The importance of managing resources
- Creation and interpretation of financial forecasts
- Viability of a business
- Demonstration of business skills/IT skills
- Producing a formal report (pages 122–125; 136)
- Preparing presentation slides and speaker notes that summarise the viability of a business plan or proposal (pages 126–128; 137).

Links To help you revise skills that might be needed in your Unit 7 set task this Workbook contains two revisions tasks starting on pages 113 and 129. The first is guided and models good techniques, to help you develop your skills. The second gives you the opportunity to apply the skills you have developed. See the introduction on page iii for more information on features included to help you revise.

Revision task 1

To support your revision, the revision task below helps you revise the skills that might be needed in your assessed task. The revision task consists of two activities based on a task brief.

The details of the actual assessed task may change so always make sure you are up to date. Ask your tutor or check the Pearson website for the most up-to-date Sample Assessment Material to get an idea of the structure of your assessed task and what this requires of you.

Revision task brief

You are employed as an assistant to the project manager of a major retailer. You have been asked to complete this task to show your understanding of how business decisions are made.

You are required to read the scenario and documents provided and then you will be asked to reach a decision and prepare a business plan in a formal report format and some presentation slides.

On the following pages you will find information relating to a proposal to develop a chain of supermarkets in the UK by an overseas retailer. You need to consider the following information carefully to create a business plan:

- background information
- socio-economic profile of the town of Brunton
- comparative business analysis.

Make sure you read the revision task brief thoroughly. Don't be tempted to go straight to the other material in the task. Being clear on the revision task brief will ensure that you:

- fully understand what you have to do
- focus on the key points in the data and information
- produce the correct documents
- don't waste valuable time doing things that are not connected to the tasks
- maximise the opportunity to produce a high-quality response.

1. Write down the type of business that forms the basis of the task.

....

....

....

2. Write down the **two** documents you need to produce as part of your set task.

....

....

3. Give the target audience for these documents.

....

....

Revision task

You must complete ALL the activities.

You will produce two documents: a report, and a document containing presentation slides with speaker notes.

Revision activity 1

Using the information provided prepare your business plan for the new supermarket. Your business plan should include:

- rationale supported by data
- consideration of risks.

You should present your plan in the style of a formal report that could be read by the project team. Your report should be clearly structured.

Ask your tutor or check the most up-to-date Sample Assessment Material on the Pearson website to establish whether your report should be produced using word processing software in your actual set task. If you wish, you could use word processing software to complete this Workbook Revision Task.

Revision activity 2

Summarise the viability of your business plan in a way that will convince the project team.

Prepare a maximum of four presentation slides to promote your summary effectively. Your slides should have brief speaker notes.

Ask your tutor or check the most up-to-date Sample Assessment Material on the Pearson website to establish whether your presentation should be produced using presentation software in your actual set task. If you wish, you could use presentation software to complete this Workbook Revision Task.

Background information

A Danish retailer, Value Supermarkets, plans to develop a chain of supermarkets in major UK towns. It is in the process of deciding the location of its first supermarket in the UK. The retailer's project team has identified the town of Brunton as a possible site.

You have researched Brunton's profile and discovered

(i) Brunton's town centre has yet to live up to its potential with the limited number of high-quality new premises failing to meet the requirements of many businesses.
(ii) There are currently no major supermarkets in Brunton town centre but there is a large hypermarket, Bestco plc, based in the Brunton Retail Park which is located six miles from the town centre.
(iii) The local council has received financial support from central government to redevelop the town centre. Planning restrictions will be imposed on any further development of the Brunton Retail Park.
(iv) There are still a significant number of unemployed people who live in Brunton but the percentage of employed adults has gone down by over 10% in the last four years.
(v) Brunton has a number of residents who are highly skilled but there are still a significant number of people who have low levels of qualification in the local area.
(vi) 60% of the workforce lives in Brunton; most of the population with higher level qualifications tend to work outside of Brunton.

The business strategy pursued by Value Supermarkets is based upon a business model incorporating the following features:

- selling high volumes of low-cost groceries (known as 'limited assortment stores')
- preference for purchasing or refurbishing existing business premises in town centres
- an international reputation for supporting community-based projects and promoting employment opportunities for older workers.

The project manager has provided you with the following sales and profits projections for the first year of operation of the new UK store assuming no financial support from the local council:

- Target annual sales turnover of the new store: £8.5 million
- Target gross profit margin: 20%
- Target net profit margin: 12%
- Tax rate: 20% of profits
- 60% of post-tax profits are distributed to shareholders

In addition, you have researched Brunton's socio-economic profile and carried out a comparative business analysis of Value Supermarkets and Bestco (see below).

You will need to decide whether you think Brunton will be a suitable location for the supermarket, and clearly make your case to the project team.

Socio-economic profile of Brunton

Table 1: Percentage growth forecasts for occupations in Brunton, 2016–22

Category	% growth
Managers	15.8
Retail and customer service	13.2
Professional occupations	6.1
Administration and secretarial	1.2

Table 2: Changes in employment by sector: Forecasts for Brunton, 2016–22

Category	% change
Public administration	−7.1%
Education	−7.2%
Financial services	+7.5%
Construction	+9.1%
Retail	+12.6%
Business services including distribution and IT services	+35.2%

Table 3: Population statistics for Brunton, 2015

Age	Actual number	% of total population	Wages as a % of UK national average wage
Total population	282 415	–	
0–14	48 575	17.2	–
15–24	83 313	29.5	76%
25–64	148 268	52.5	72%
65+	2259	0.8	–

Table 4: Analysis of Brunton workforce, 2014

Feature	Percentage of total Brunton workforce
Employment of the working age population	78.4%
Benefit claimants	11.0%
Percentage of working population with no qualifications	8.1%

Comparative business analysis (Value Supermarkets and Bestco plc)

Table 5: Product ranges

	Number of product lines	
Type of product range	**BESTCO plc**	**Value Supermarkets**
Premium quality range	200 (19 %)	20 (0.02%)
Organic range	200 (5%)	50 (0.5%)
Traditional grocery range	1000 (62%)	–
Low-cost range	200 (8%)	1100 (99.48 %)
Healthy options	100 (3%)	–
Clothing range	100 (2%)	–
Consumer electronics	50 (1%)	–

Notes:
(i) Figures in brackets show the percentage value of the total sales generated in each product range category.
(ii) Bestco plc also operates a financial services division which provides banking services including credit cards and personal loans.

Table 6: Business features

Business feature	BESTCO plc	Value Supermarkets
Countries	Operates in UK with stores throughout the EU and the Far East	Denmark, France and Germany
Routes to market	High street stores Online grocery ordering	High street stores only
Portfolio	Groceries Financial services Electrical goods Clothing In-store cafes	Low-cost groceries Limited product range Special one-off price offers
Customer retention	65%	80%
Market share in the UK (2015)	28%	–
% change in UK market share over the last 5 years	–4%	–
Inventory turnover	**8** *(i)* **6** *(ii)*	**10** *(i)*

Notes:
(i) Food grocery items
(ii) Non-food products

Revision activity 1

Using the information provided prepare your business plan for the new supermarket. Your business plan should include:

- rationale supported by data
- consideration of risks.

You should present your plan in the style of a formal report that could be read by the project team. Your report should be clearly structured.

Ask your tutor or check the most up-to-date Sample Assessment Material on the Pearson website to establish whether your report should be produced using word processing software in your actual set task. If you wish, you could use word processing software to complete this Revision Workbook Task.

Now that you have familiarised yourself with what you have to do and carefully read through the background information, look to see if there are any **calculations** that you can complete from the **data** which you can use in your report or presentation. You also need to consider if there are any **inferences** or **conclusions** you can draw from the **written information**.

Guided

Calculate the following key **financial performance indicators**:

(a) Total annual gross profit from the new store

Gross profit = Turnover × gross profit margin

.... = 20% of £ .... = £ ....

(b) Total annual net profit from the store

....

(c) Amount paid in tax

....

(d) Total amount of funds distributed to shareholders

....

(e) Total amount of net profit retained by Value Supermarkets

....

Guided

You will need to use the information about Value Supermarket's business strategy when making a judgement on the suitability of Brunton as the location of the new store. Write down three key words or phrases which you could use to sum up the business strategy at Value Supermarkets:

1. high volume

2. ....

3. ....

One approach you could take to analyse Brunton's town profile is to identify how each feature within the town profile can add value to Value Supermarkets' business strategy. The town profile can also be the starting point for identifying any potential business risks for Value Supermarkets if it decides to locate in Brunton. Remember that business risks may still exist even in those instances where you identify potential business advantages.

1. Review each of the features identified in the Brunton town profile and write a short statement about how each feature could either **add value to**, or **detract from**, the business strategy at Value Supermarkets.

....

....

....

....

....

2. List any potential business risks which may impact on the business strategy at Value Supermarkets based on the information provided in the Brunton town profile.

....

....

....

....

Links An external environmental analysis can be conducted using a PESTLE analysis – see the Revision Guide, page 19.

Value Supermarkets will need to recruit, train and pay people to work in its new store. It is therefore important to undertake a provisional **labour market analysis**. The purpose of this analysis is to determine if there will be any potential recruitment issues should Value Supermarkets decide to open a store in Brunton. This labour market analysis can also be used to identify potential business risks.

You need to distinguish between **factual numbers** and **forecasts**. Which two tables on pages 116–117 represent actual data?

.... and ....

Links For help with **labour market analysis**, see the Revision Guide, pages 99–103.

1. Look at Table 1 on page 116.

   (a) Why do you think there is such a high growth forecast in retail and customer service occupations?

....

....

....

....

(b) Are there any potential risks for Value Supermarkets in the growth in management occupations?

Refer back to the Brunton town profile on page 115.

....

....

....

....

2. Look at Table 2 on page 116.

(a) Describe any features which indicate that economic activity in the local economy is likely to increase over the period 2016–22.

Look at the type of employment categories which are forecast to increase.

....

....

....

....

(b) Identify any potential opportunities or risks for Value Supermarkets in these sector employment forecasts.

Value Supermarkets will need to recruit people who require to be managed. They will also need an efficient distribution network to receive supplies and distribute goods should they develop an online shopping platform.

....

....

....

....

....

3. Look at Table 3 on page 116.

Explain what the table tells us about the general level of wages in the Brunton area and identify any potential issues for Value Supermarkets.

Consider labour costs and the level of local consumer demand.

....

....

....

....

4. Look at Table 4 on page 116.

What opportunities exist for Value Supermarkets to demonstrate its corporate social responsibility in Brunton?

Refer back to Value Supermarkets' business strategy on page 115.

....

....

....

....

Analyse the data in **Tables 5 and 6** on page 117, along with any other relevant data provided in the background information sheets, and complete a competitor analysis of Bestco plc.

In Table 5 consider factors such as:

- The product ranges offered by each supermarket – how does a wide product range give a business a competitive advantage over its rivals?
- What advantages and disadvantages does specialisation bring to a business?

In Table 6 consider the following in your analysis:

- Are there any factors which could give one business a competitive advantage over the other?
- Are there any potential 'warning signs' which may impact upon future business performance?

A competitor analysis will seek to identify the main competitors in a market along with their strengths and weaknesses. Analysing the results of a competitor analysis will enable a business to establish a strategy which includes elements such as the products to be offered, the price of the product and the location of the business.

....

....

....

....

....

....

....

....

....

....

....

....

....

....

....

....

....

Links You can find more on competitor analysis in the Revision Guide, page 137. Value Supermarkets will have to have a clear understanding of the business risks involved in their proposed new venture. SWOT and PESTLE analyses are useful ways of identifying these risks. You can find information on these in the Revision Guide, page 19.

Now that you have completed your analysis of the background information, use the space below to write the business plan for the new supermarket. Remember to write your plan in the style of a formal report. If you wish, you can word process your report.

Revision activity 1

Now write your **Activity 1** report (see page 118). Your report should have a title and date. Make sure you include your name and the intended recipient of the report and its status.

Guided

Formal report on Brunton proposal

Date: ....

Recommendation for discussion

This report has been compiled by .... and is intended for the Project Manager.

1. Introduction

Your report should be well planned and have a logical structure. You should start your report with an introduction (or executive summary) and then divide the main body of the report into four to six sections using main headings and sub-headings. For example, you may decide to include a main section heading such as 'Brunton' which could be subdivided into 'Local economic profile' and 'Labour market analysis'. Some of the other possible headings you could use in your report are:

- Financial targets
- Brunton location
- Labour market analysis
- Competitor analysis
- Risk analysis
- Conclusions and recommendations.

Look back at the work you did on pages 118–121.

The purpose of this report is ....

....

....

....

....

Financial targets

It is important to understand the key financial performance indicators for the proposed expansion into Brunton. We are aiming to generate an annual gross profit of £........................ on annual sales turnover of £8.5 million. This represents a 20% gross profit margin. A target net profit margin of 12% means annual net profits will be £........................ .

Make sure you include any relevant performance indicators that you have calculated.

Links For a reminder on how to calculate profitability ratios – gross profit margin and net profit margin – see the Revision Guide, pages 76–77. You may be provided with an income statement or a statement of financial position in the actual set task, in which case you will also need to calculate liquidity and performance ratios. You can revise ratio analysis on pages 76–80 of the Revision Guide.

3. Brunton location

The advantages of the proposed Brunton location are ....

....

The disadvantages of the proposed Brunton location are

For each main area that you cover in your report, you should include:
- Strengths (benefits)
- Weaknesses (risks)
- Opportunities
- Threats

4. Labour market analysis

Write up the results of your labour market analysis in this section of the report.

The latest figures show that 74.8% of the workforce are currently in work.

You might wish to support your business plan with **charts** and **diagrams**. Make sure any charts or diagrams:
- have a title
- are relevant to your analysis
- help to justify your conclusions
- enhance the rationale of the business case you are presenting.

The chart shows the percentage growth forecasts for occupations in Brunton over the period 2016–22.

The expansion into Brunton will provide opportunities for Value Supermarkets to demonstrate corporate social responsibility, such as

Remember your formal report is for a business audience (the project team). You should use appropriate **business language** throughout.

5. Competitor analysis

The competitor analysis in this report is based on the available data of a major supermarket, Bestco plc.

....

....

....

....

6. SWOT and PESTLE analyses

Remember to include the risks you have identified. You need only include the analysis at this stage of your report. Save any recommendations for the final section of your report.

....

....

....

....

....

....

....

....

....

....

7. Conclusions and recommendations

This report finds that Brunton .... a suitable location for Value Supermarkets.

You need to decide whether you are going to recommend Brunton as a suitable location. Write 'is' or 'is not' in the space above. Remember to **justify** your conclusion with reference to the data.

....

....

....

....

....

....

....

....

....

....

Links There is more support on how to prepare a formal report in the Revision Guide, page 124.

Revision activity 2

Summarise your findings in a way that will convince the project team whether to locate in Brunton.

Prepare a maximum of four presentation slides to promote your summary effectively. Your slides should have brief speaker notes.

Use the space below to outline your four slides, and to write your speaker notes.

Ask your tutor or check the most up-to-date Sample Assessment Material on the Pearson website to establish whether you will create your slides and notes using presentation software. If you wish, you could create your slides and notes using presentation software for this Revision Workbook Task.

Use the space below to outline your four slides, and to write your speaker notes. Each slide should have a title so think carefully about what your four slides should be. Here are four possible titles for your slides:

- Brunton profile
- Competitor profile – Bestco plc
- Risk analysis
- Opportunities for Value Supermarkets in Brunton

Guided

Slide 1

1. Brunton – profile

- Population 282 415
- No major supermarkets in the town centre
- ....
- ....
- ....
- ....
- ....

Slide 1 speaker notes

- Town centre will be redeveloped (with financial aid)
- Planning restrictions to be imposed on developments in the retail park (Bestco plc is the main local supermarket located in the retail park)
- Summary of workforce data (8.1% no quals; 11% benefit claimants)
- ....
- ....
- ....
- ....
- ....

Your slides should clearly **summarise** the information given in your formal report. If each slide contains **too much information** or **too many graphics**, your presentation might be difficult to understand. Choose **important information** to put on the slide, then expand on it in the speaker notes.

Speaker notes should be **brief**. You are not expected to write down everything the speaker will say. You can keep your speaker notes short by presenting them as **bullet points**. Speaker notes do not simply contain the same information as is given on the slide. They can include additional information and data that the speaker will provide during his or her presentation.

Links Further guidance on creating business presentations can be found in the Revision Guide on page 125.

Slide 2

....
- ....
- ....
- ....
- ....
- ....
- ....

Slide 2 speaker notes

- ....
- ....
- ....
- ....
- ....
- ....
- ....

Slides 2 and 3 should cover:
- competitor profile
- risk analysis
- the main issues.

Use six to seven points per slide and simple graphics where necessary. Include a heading in each slide.

Use the speaker notes to provide some of the detail to back up the presentation and to point out some of the issues.

Slide 3

....
- ....
- ....
- ....
- ....
- ....
- ....

Slide 3 speaker notes

- ....
- ....
- ....
- ....
- ....
- ....

Slide 4

....

- ....
- ....
- ....
- ....

....

....

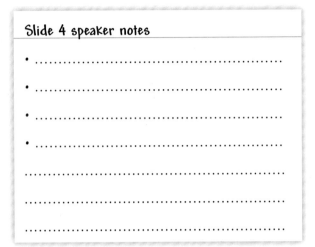

Slide 4 speaker notes

- ....
- ....
- ....
- ....

....

....

....

The final slide should provide a summary of the opportunities for Value Supermarkets of locating in Brunton.

Include three or four main conclusions.

Finish with a question to capture the audience's attention.

Use the speaker notes to explain why these are the important conclusions.

Links There is more support on preparing presentation slides and speaker notes in the Revision Guide on page 168.

Revision task 2

To support your revision, the revision task below helps you revise the skills that might be needed in your assessed task. The revision task consists of two activities based on a task brief.

The details of the actual assessed task may change so always make sure you are up to date. Ask your tutor or check the Pearson website for the most up-to-date Sample Assessment Material to get an idea of the structure of your assessed task and what this requires of you.

Revision task brief

You are employed as an assistant to the owner of a small business. You have been asked to complete this task to show your understanding of how business decisions are made.

You are required to read the scenario and documents provided and then you will be asked to reach a decision and prepare a business plan in a formal report format and some presentation slides.

On the following pages you will find information relating to a small construction business which is proposing to seek capital investment. You need to consider the following information carefully to create a business plan:

- background information
- email from the owner of the construction company
- income statement
- statement of financial position
- information on proposed capital investment
- cash flow forecast
- article from the local newspaper.

Revision task

Revision activity 1

Using the information provided, prepare your business plan for the proposed capital investment. Your business plan should include:

- rationale supported by data
- consideration of risks.

You should present your plan in the style of a formal report that could be read by the owner of the business and potential investors. Your report should be clearly structured.

Ask your tutor or check the most up-to-date Sample Assessment Material on the Pearson website to establish whether your report should be produced using word processing software in your actual set task. If you wish, you could use word processing software to complete this Revision Workbook Task.

Revision activity 2

Summarise the viability of your business plan in a way that will convince the owner and potential investors.

Prepare a maximum of four presentation slides to promote your summary effectively. Your slides should have brief speaker notes.

Ask your tutor or check the most up-to-date Sample Assessment Material on the Pearson website to establish whether your presentation should be produced using presentation software in your actual set task. If you wish, you could use presentation software to complete this Revision Workbook Task.

Background information

Ashbury Construction was established ten years ago. The company supplies tools and building materials for the construction industry. Before making any further capital investment into the company the owner has decided to have a review of the business. The capital investment will require access to external business finance and he has been advised by a small business adviser to put together a business plan.

The owner has asked you to look at some additional financial information to help him assess the performance of his business and prepare a business plan.

Email from the owner of Ashbury Construction

To: A. Learner
From: Ron Nayall

Thanks for agreeing to help me review the business. Can you have a look at the attached documents and let me know how I could use the information to assess how well the company is performing which can be included in a business plan?

I'm thinking of investing in some new equipment used on construction sites. My plan is to grow the business by hiring out equipment to local builders. To start off I've looked at purchasing a generator. I'm considering two models but I'm not sure which one would be better for the business in terms of maximising returns. I've also done a cash flow forecast for the next year although I did this in a bit of a rush!

I've got an appointment with the bank's Small Business Advisor next week so it would be really helpful if you could put together a draft business plan in a report format and let me have your thoughts about my proposal.

Thanks

Ron

Make sure you have a clear idea of Ron's business strategy and look for some key pointers which Ron needs help on – they'll form the basis of the documents you need to prepare.

Ashbury Construction:
Income Statement for year ended 31 December

	£	£
Sales		200 000
Less cost of goods sold		
Opening stock	5 000	
Purchases	85 000	
Less closing stock	10 000	
		80 000
Gross profit		120 000
Less expenses		
Lighting and heating	5 000	
Wages	40 000	
Vehicle expenses	8 000	
Office expenses	47 000	100 000
Net profit		20 000

Ashbury Construction:
Statement of Financial Position for year ended 31 December

	£	£
Capital: At start		65 000
Add net profit		20 000
		85 000
Less drawings		12 000
		73 000
Represented by:		
Fixed assets:		
Vehicle	20 000	
Plant and equipment	18 000	38 000
Current assets:		
Inventory (stock)	10 000	
Debtors	20 000	
Bank	15 000	
Cash	5 000	
	50 000	
Less current liabilities:		
Creditors	15 000	
Net working capital		35 000
		73 000

Think about what information you can extract directly from these financial statements that will influence business decisions. What calculations could you perform to identify the financial viability of the business?

Proposed capital investment

Ron Nayall wants to purchase one of the following generators which he will hire out to local construction companies.

The Titan 100 generator costs £40 000 or can be leased over a three-year period with an initial payment of £4000 followed by 36 monthly payments of £350. Processing fee £199.

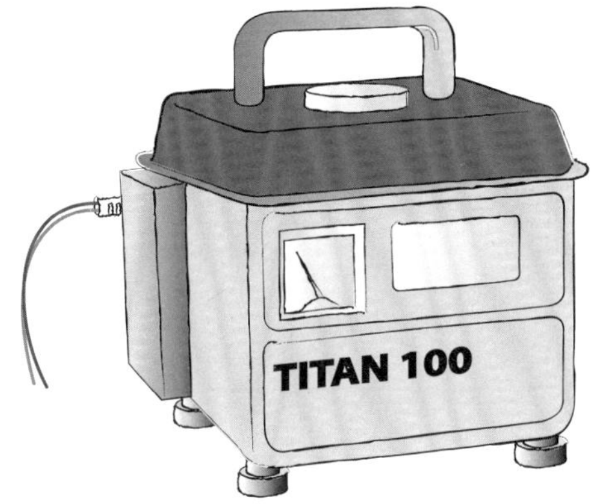

The Titan 500 generator costs £56 000 or can be leased over a two-year period with an initial payment of £6000 followed by 24 monthly payments of £450. Processing fee £199.

The company plans to replace the machines with newer models after five years. The *Titan 100* generator is a smaller, cheaper version of the *Titan 500* and the company will be able to hire it out immediately to its existing customers. To make use of the larger *Titan 500* generator will require Ashbury Construction to negotiate contracts with larger construction companies.

Ron Nayall has predicted the extra business the machines will generate over the next five years.

	The *Titan 100* generator		The *Titan 500* generator	
Year	**Cash outflow**	**Cash inflow**	**Cash outflow**	**Cash inflow**
0	40 000		56 000	
1		24 000		20 000
2		16 000		20 000
3		10 000		18 000
4		8 000		18 000
5		4 000		10 000
		62 000		86 000

Net present value table

	Present value of £1	
Year	**5%**	**10%**
1	0.952	0.909
2	0.907	0.826
3	0.860	0.751
4	0.823	0.683
5	0.780	0.621

Think about whether Ron should lease or buy the equipment and how calculating net present value can assist capital investment decisions.

Cash flow forecast

	Jan	Feb	Mar	Apr	May	Jun	Jul	Aug	Sept	Oct	Nov	Dec
Income												
Sales	12000	14000	14000	17000	17000	18000	19000	18000	17000	13000	11000	9000
Equipment hire	2000	2000	2000	2000	2000	2000	2000	2000	2000	2000	2000	2000
Total income	14000	16000	16000	19000	19000	20000	21000	20000	19000	15000	13000	11000
Expenditure												
Inventory (stock)	8000	12000	12000	11000	8000	7000	7000	6000	6000	6000	6000	6000
Business rates			400			400			400			400
Insurance				1100								
Heating and lighting				2000				500				1000
Wages	2000	2500	3000	3000	4000	4000	4000	3000	2500	2500	2000	2000
Advertising	500	200	1500	1000	200	200	200	200	200	200	200	200
Vehicle expenses			1000			1000			1000			1000
Administration	50	50	50	50	50	50	50	50	50	50	50	50
Loan repayments	1000	1000	1000	1000	1000	1000	1000	1000	1000	1000	1000	1000
Total expenditure	11550	15750	18950	19150	13250	13650	12250	10750	11150	9750	9250	11650
Income – expenditure	2450	250	–2950	–150	5750	6350	8750	9250	7850	5250	3750	–650
Balance b/f		2450	2700	250	100	5850	12200	20950	30200	38050	43300	47050

Will the business generate sufficient cash? Why is it important to be cautious about interpreting cash flow forecasts?

Article in local newspaper

Council rejects 300 houses in Ploughfield

Local builders were left disappointed when, at last night's Council meeting, planning permission was refused for the construction of 300 new houses in the Ploughfield area of the town. The decision was welcomed by local residents who had objected to houses being built on a greenfield site.

Edgware Construction plc would have been the main contractor and local builders were hoping that the company would sub-contract most of the work.

Plans have already been approved for Edgware Construction plc to build 600 low-cost housing units on the brownfield site situated to the east of the borough although, following the outcome of last night's meeting, there are rumours that Edgware Construction plc may be considering alternative sites in different parts of the country.

Shares in Edgware Construction plc have been under pressure since the start of the year as a result of the downturn in the economy and the outcome of last night's meeting did nothing to dispel rumours that one of its major competitors is considering launching a take-over bid for the company.

Business decisions involve risks. What risks can you identify in this article which may impact on Ashbury Construction?

Do these risks mean that you would advise against expanding the business?

Can you identify any potential business opportunities?

Revision activity 1

Using the information provided, prepare your business plan for the proposed capital investment. Your business plan should include:

- rationale supported by data
- consideration of risks.

You should present your plan in the style of a formal report that could be read by the owner of the business and potential investors. Your report should be clearly structured.

Ask your tutor or check the most up-to-date Sample Assessment Material on the Pearson website to establish whether your report should be produced using word processing software in your actual set task. If you wish, you could use word processing software to complete this Revision Workbook Task.

Now that you have completed your analysis of the background information, use this page to write the business plan for proposed capital investment. Remember to write your plan in the style of a formal report. Number each of the sections in your business plan and give each section a heading. If you wish, you can word process your report.

Start your business plan with the background to the business proposal, some high-level financial performance indicators, the opportunities for profit and why the business needs additional finance.

Providers of business finance, as well as potential investors, will want to be reassured that the plan is realistic. Including a risk analysis will show that you have thought about all aspects of the plan.

Continue your report on separate sheets of paper.

Revision activity 2

Summarise the viability of your business plan in a way that will convince the owner and potential investors.

Prepare a maximum of four presentation slides to promote your summary effectively. Your slides should have brief speaker notes.

> Ask your tutor or check the most up-to-date Sample Assessment Material on the Pearson website to establish whether your presentation should be produced using presentation software in your actual set task. If you wish, you could use presentation software to complete this Revision Workbook Task.

Use the space below to outline your four slides, and to write your speaker notes. If you wish, you can use presentation software. Each slide should have a title so think carefully about what your four slides should be.

....

- ....
- ....
- ....
- ....
- ....

Slide 1 speaker notes

- ....
- ....
- ....
- ....
- ....

....

- ....
- ....
- ....
- ....
- ....

Slide 2 speaker notes

- ....
- ....
- ....
- ....
- ....

....

- ....
- ....
- ....
- ....
- ....

Slide 3 speaker notes

- ....
- ....
- ....
- ....
- ....

....

- ....
- ....
- ....
- ....
- ....

Slide 4 speaker notes

- ....
- ....
- ....
- ....
- ....

Links There is more support on preparing presentation slides and speaker notes in the Revision Guide on page 168.

Answers

Unit 2: Developing a Marketing Campaign

Revision task 1 (pages 2–33)

Revision activity 1

Summary of marketing campaign's rationale (pages 21–22)

Learners will produce their own individual rationale based on the scenario, the information provided and personal research. Individual responses will vary, but may consider the following:
Product: designing, creating, branding and marketing the new gyms to the target market
Promotion: how the new gyms will be marketed, for example through advertising, social media
Pricing: how pricing strategies for membership of the gyms, products and services will be decided
Place: how products and services offered by the gym will be available to customers at a time and place to suit their needs.

Marketing aims and objectives (pages 23–24)

Individual responses. You may identify a range of marketing aims and objectives for John's Gyms. Below are some possible marketing aims and objectives, but there may be many others.

- Inform target audience about features and benefits of John's Gyms within six months.
- Increase brand awareness of John's Gyms in London by 30% within two years.
- Increase gym membership to 300 members per gym within two years.
- Gain 10% market share of London's fitness and gym market within three years.
- Increase sales revenue from the three London gyms to £300,000 with three years.

Individual responses. You should explain how each of your marketing aims and objectives will be achieved. Your objectives should be SMART.

Research data on the market and competition (pages 25–27)

Individual responses. You will have undertaken your own research and made notes on pages 14–19. Refer also to the sample research notes provided on these pages.

Justification for my rationale (pages 27–28)

Individual responses, with rationale and justification based on the scenario, information provided and personal research into a marketing campaign of your choice. The sample response of one approach below can be used to review your own work, for example.
The aims and objectives set for John's Gyms are appropriate as he is entering a new market and therefore needs to let people know about his product in order to achieve market share and increase gym memberships. John will also be making a lot of investment in the new gyms and the marketing campaign and therefore it is important that he generates sales revenue to pay this money back. Customers need to know about the gyms' features and benefits so they understand their unique selling points and join the gyms. John's Gyms is a profit-making business and John wants to expand his business. To do this he must make sure that the London gyms are successful.
The target market for the gyms are people on middle incomes who live in or close to the city. They are John's core market in the north of England and therefore he has experience in working with this group of people. My research has told me that there has been a growth in the market for low-cost gyms in London so it might not be a good idea to target solely at this type of customer, as this part of the market will already be taken by other gyms such as The Gym Group. However, I think it would be a good idea to offer a pay-as-you-go package for those people who cannot afford a membership fee.
My research has told me that there is a lot of competition in London as there are a lot of gyms. Therefore it is important to ensure that John creates a really good brand image early on so that people get to know his business and like to go to his gyms. My research from the report on gyms and fitness centres in the UK also tells me that people like to do other types of fitness activities such as Zumba classes and boot camps, so I think it is important for John to offer these services as well as the usual facilities, such as gym equipment, a swimming pool and shop. I also think he should offer a personal trainer service for those people who are either new to gyms or want to train seriously. As the case study tells me that John's Gyms are aimed at men and women, it is important to offer facilities and services that appeal to both. Men tend to like equipment that builds muscles, such as weight machines and also things like circuit training, so John should offer this and aim it at men. Women like to tone and socialise, so classes like Zumba would be good, as this might appeal to them. John might also need to offer a children's area so they can play while their parents work out.
London is a very crowded place and therefore the marketing campaign must be targeted towards areas where people travel and can see information easily. Adverts at bus stops etc. would be a really good idea as a lot of people use public transport in London. I think you could also use leaflets handed out in the city centre to promote the business. TV adverts are really expensive so aren't really an option, as the case study tells me that he only has £150,000 for the marketing campaign, but I think if the business proves successful, then John could use TV advertising in future.
John will need to think carefully about pricing, as research from *The Economist* shows that the average price of gym membership in London is between £15.99 and £70: he can't charge too much, but needs to charge enough to cover his costs and also make a profit.
I think my timescale of initially three years is appropriate as it is enough time to start to break even and make some profit, and it is long enough to decide if the gyms in London will be a success.

Revision activity 2

The marketing mix (pages 29–32)
Individual responses, with the marketing campaign based on your responses to Revision activity 1 and personal research. The sample response of one approach below can be used to review your own work, for example.
Product development
John's Gyms will be aimed at middle-income people living or working in London. The case study tells me that John already works with this market in the north of England and therefore he understands what he wants. Also, my research from ONS tells me that areas such as Wandsworth, Islington, Hammersmith & Fulham, Camden and Kingston upon Thames, for example, have average incomes of between £30 000 and £35 000 and therefore the middle-income market is the best idea for John's Gyms. The gyms should be open between 6am and 10pm every day, but on Monday–Thursday there will need to be more staff as these are the most popular days. Similarly, 6am–8am, 12pm–2pm and 6pm–8pm are the most popular times of the day (research from the PT Direct website tells me this) and therefore more staff will be needed at these times as well.
During the day and in the early evenings, a personal fitness trainer service will be offered for those people who want more help in their training regimes. As a lot of women like to visit the gym during the day, John's Gyms will offer classes such as Zumba during the day and also in the early evening for those women who work. There will also be a children's play area so the children can play while their parents are at the gym. Fitness equipment such as running machines and weight-lifting machines will be provided at all times and the swimming pool

will be available all day every day, offering some swimming lessons at the weekends. John's Gyms will also offer one-hour boot camps on Monday and Thursday evenings and in the afternoon at weekends. My research using the 'Report on gym and fitness centres in the UK' tells me that these are popular. John's Gyms should offer memberships ranging from £50–£70 depending on the level of service, and other classes will be charged individually. There will also be the opportunity to offer a pay-as-you-go service during quieter times such as between 2pm and 6pm on weekdays and at the weekend.

I would look at creating a brand image which is related to how people will want to look at the end of going to the gym. Therefore, promotional displays and advertisements would show muscly men and attractive, toned women. The overall image for John's Gyms would be around young middle-income people having fun and getting fit but working this around busy lifestyles, as my research from the ONS tells me that the group of people with the highest population in London are aged between 20 and 39 years old. The case study also tells me that one in eight people are members of a gym so I know that John's Gyms could be successful.

Pricing strategies

John's Gyms should offer a membership fee of between £50 and £70. The £50 membership fee will be an off-peak membership whereas the £70 membership fee would be at any time. In addition to this, at quiet times such as between 2pm and 6pm, when demand for the gyms falls, John could offer a £5 pay-as-you-go fee. Personal training will be offered at an additional £25 per hour and classes such as Zumba will be £8 for each session.

These prices are based on competitive pricing as research has shown me that the average price of gym membership in London is between £19.99 and £90. The price is therefore within this range and is going for middle incomes. The pay-as-you-go price will also appeal to those people on lower incomes. The personal training and class prices are based on cost-plus pricing as John needs to see that these are profitable or he shouldn't run them.

These prices will allow John to reach his target market of middle-income people working in London. If John achieves his target of 300 customers per gym in two years' time and they all pay the full £70 membership fee, this would mean that he will make over £60 000 just from membership fees and therefore could start to make some profit. He also needs to enter the market so the price of the membership and services could rise in the future to make more profit.

Promotion and selection of media

John should use the following to promote his gyms:

- Leaflets to be handed out in the areas where the gyms are set up. They would use the images suggested of muscly men and attractive, toned women having fun and getting fit as this is the brand image I have selected for the gym. My research tells me that I can get 1000 leaflets for £19.99 from VistaPrint and therefore I could get 100 000 leaflets initially for £1999.99. This would need to be done a month before the gyms open and then repeated once each month for the first six months. John would also need to pay someone to hand them out on minimum wage.
- I would also look at advertising in a daily regional newspaper in London two weeks before the gyms open which would cost me £500 per advert for a half page (source: Marketing Minefield). This would cost £5000 for this two-week period and then I would suggest a quarter-page advert a week for the next 12 months which costs £12 500.
- The weekend before the opening of the gym and for three weeks afterwards, John should run an advert on a regional radio station. My research from radioadvertising.co.uk shows that a 30-second advert for a week on a regional radio station would cost £2500. This would therefore cost John £10 000. He should continue this one week in every month for six months.
- Social media is one of the fastest and cheapest methods of reaching customers as campaigns can quickly go viral and attract huge amounts of interest in a company. By getting likes/shares for an opportunity to win a trial membership, John can build up a database of target customers. John should run a simple social media campaign for 12 months starting before the opening of the gym. This would cost £150 for set-up costs and £3000 for 12 months.
- As London is a place where many people use public transport, it would be a good idea to advertise on bus stops around the locations of the three gyms. I would advise using five bus stops in all three locations for two weeks before the opening, and then two weeks in every month for six months. My research from marketingdonut.co.uk shows this would cost £300 per bus stop advert for two weeks and therefore this would cost £31 500.
- I would also use billboard advertising in one location near each gym for one month before and six months after the gyms open. This costs £200 for a 48-sheet billboard per week (marketingdonut.co.uk) and therefore total cost will be £16 800.
- As John already has gyms in the north of England, he should already have a website and therefore could add the three new gyms to this website for free.

Place

The three gyms need to be set up where people have average middle incomes – this is the target market for the gyms. I would therefore suggest that John locates the gyms in either Wandsworth, Islington, Hammersmith & Fulham, Camden or Kingston upon Thames as my research for the ONS tells me that this is where average incomes are between £30 000 and £35 000. The gyms need to be in the town centres, with access to parking and with sufficient space to accommodate the gym including a swimming pool. They should also be close to local parks for the boot camps to take place. It would also be a good idea to locate the gyms near Tube stations where possible to make them easy to get to as a lot of people travel by public transport in London. However, John will need to consider the price of the location so he does not pick one that is too expensive.

Extended marketing mix (page 33)

People – John would need to make sure that he trains his staff to provide good customer service. They would need some induction training to ensure that they know how to do this. He will also recruit personal trainers. It would be good if he could find ones with good reputations.

Physical environment – It is important that John makes his gyms attractive with images related to the brand image I have suggested. Pictures of muscly men and attractive, toned women should be displayed around the gym. It is also important that the gym is the correct temperature and is kept clean and tidy.

Processes – I would suggest that John invests in an electronic sign-in system which scans people's fingers in order to get into the gym. This would be efficient and means that there would be fewer staff but is expensive. He also needs to create a database of customers which includes a booking system for the additional services offered.

Budget (page 32)

Total spend

£1999.99	initial leaflets
£5000	initial newspaper advert
£12 500	newspaper adverts for 12 months
£10 000	initial regional radio advertising
£15 000	6 months' regional radio advertising
£3150	12 months' social media advertising
£31 500	Bus stop advertising
£16 800	Billboard advertising

Total = £95 949.99

This leaves £54 050.01 from the budget. John will need to pay someone to give out leaflets and this will cost £1612.80 for the first two months. John also needs to leave money left over to continue advertising after the first six months. I would advise John to review his marketing media after six months and evaluate which ones worked best and then use the remainder of the money to continue with those forms of promotion.

Timescale (page 33)

The plan costs £95 949.99 for the forms of promotion. The design of the gyms and pictures and images will also need to be considered. This plan is for the month before the gyms open and the first six months. It is important to invest in promotion before the gyms open as he is just starting out in London. He will also need to market the business heavily in the first six months in order to attract and maintain the target market.

This leaves £54 050.01 left over for use after the first six months. John needs to evaluate how successful the marketing campaign has been in meeting his marketing objectives and continue to use the mediums which have been successful.

As John's Gyms become more popular in the future, he might be able to afford TV advertising, which is too expensive initially. A TV advertising campaign ranges between £20 000 and £50 000 based on my research from info@advertising.co.uk but this is national and therefore would promote both the London gyms and the ten located in the north of England.

Evaluation (page 33)

John will know whether his marketing campaign is successful by comparing the performance of the gyms against John's marketing objectives.

- Inform target audience about features and benefits of John's Gyms within six months.
- Increase brand awareness of John's Gyms in London by 30% within two years.
- Increase gym membership to 300 members per gym within two years.
- Gain 10% market share of London's fitness and gym market within three years.
- Increase sales revenue from the three London gyms to £300 000 within three years.

Revision task 2 (pages 34–43)

For Revision task 2, you will carry out your own research and write your own notes. The responses to the revision activities that follow provide an example only, against which you can review your own work.

Revision activity 1 (page 37)

Marketing aims and objectives

Possible responses could include:

- Re-establish Henderson's Toys as a high-quality luxury toy provider within 12 months.
- Increase brand awareness of Henderson's Toys across the UK and internationally within 12 months.
- Establish the brand within the adult collectors' market within two years.
- Increase sales revenue to £2 million within 3 years.

Research data on the market and competition

Suggested sources to use:

http://www.ibisworld.co.uk/market-research/game-toy-manufacturing.html

http://www.mcvuk.com/news/read/uk-toy-industry-worth-2-96bn/090201

http://www.telegraph.co.uk/finance/newsbysector/retailandconsumer/11624459/The-UK-has-the-worlds-second-highest-spend-per-child-on-toys.html

https://uk.finance.yahoo.com/news/global-toy-market-000000679.html

http://www.economist.com/blogs/schumpeter/2013/09/toy-industry

http://www.euromonitor.com/traditional-toys-and-games-in-the-united-kingdom/report

http://www.prweb.com/releases/2013/7/prweb10927739.htm

http://www.fixedpricewebsite.co.uk/

> Remember you could use some of the key information and sources used in Revision task 1. You could use the costings provided alongside others you can find.

Possible competitors:

- Hasbro UK Ltd
- Hornby PLC
- Lego Company Ltd
- Mattel UK Ltd
- The Character Group PLC
- Amazon UK

Possible pieces of information to include:

- Population figures in Yorkshire, the UK and the world
- Statistics on market share, sales revenues and profits in the toys and games industry
- Trends in sales and popular toys and games
- Prices of other manufacturers' products
- Costings from alternative suppliers
- PESTLE information, including economic data and legislation impacting on the industry
- Information on key competitors in the UK and internationally
- Information on other companies' websites and e-commerce

Evaluation of the reliability and validity of the information researched:

See examples in the response to Revision task 1 on pages 25–27.

Justification

Possible responses include:

- The aims and objectives are appropriate for Henderson's Toys as the business is in decline and therefore needs to boost sales and diversify.
- It is important that they generate more sales revenue in order to continue to operate in the market.
- Other suppliers need to be researched as they have increased their prices by between 10% and 15%.
- They need to look into new markets as there is fierce competition from foreign-made toys and games, especially from Asia.
- Their core target market is both boys and girls aged 2–8 years old but they need to look into aiming at the lucrative adult collectors' market as well.
- As UK parents spend on average £508 on toys per child each year, they need to focus on middle-class households.
- They need to focus on the niche high-quality luxury toy market as there has been a change in the toys and games sold.
- As the designs and specifications have changed little over time, this may need to be reviewed or traditional needs to be their unique selling point.
- As the local market has more competition from cheaper imported toys, Henderson's Toys should look at distributing across the world using the internet and e-commerce. As they only have £75 000 in their marketing budget, this is all the more important as this form of marketing could be very low cost.
- As they have experienced a decline in sales revenue over the past ten years and are facing fierce competition, the timescale needs to be short as they need to turn the business around quickly.

Revision activity 2 (page 40)

Possible responses could include:

Product development

- Henderson's Toys should concentrate on their core bestselling products of handmade teddy bears, dolls and wooden toys.
- They should focus still on the company as a high-quality brand, aimed at the middle- and higher-income markets.
- Their unique selling point is the quality of their products and the traditional design.
- New designs focusing on recent trends and fashions could also be developed under another related brand name and image.
- The high-quality product means that they can charge a premium price, selling the products in retailers such as Hamleys and over the internet.
- The products are currently in saturation or decline in the product life cycle and therefore the aim of this marketing campaign is to push them back to maturity.
- The products could be re-packaged to be attractive to the adult collectors' market alongside the original packaging aimed at children aged 2–8 years old.
- The website could be used to allow customers to 'build a toy' which would result in bespoke toys at a premium price.

Pricing strategies

- The products should be priced between £25 and £100. The cheaper toys would be small dolls, trains and small teddy bears. The more expensive toys would be handmade china luxury dolls, dolls houses, teddy families and complete train sets.
- A further supplement would be charged for the 'build a toy' service of between £5 and £40 pounds depending on the number of alterations made to the core product.
- Skimming could be used to result in a premium price to match the high-quality image.
- However, the costs of the raw materials need to be considered due to high supplier costs and therefore there would be an element of cost-plus pricing.

Promotion and selection of media

- A website could be created to promote the company and provide access to e-commerce. A website could cost as little as £399 to set up.
- Henderson's Toys could use online distributors such as eBay and Amazon to sell their products.
- Advertisements could be put in national newspapers such as the *Daily Mail* each weekend for 12 months. However, a full page costs over £30 000 and therefore a much smaller advert would be required costing approximately £3000 per advert.
- Advertisements could be placed in specialist toy magazines aimed at the adult collectors' market each fortnight for £200 per advert.
- TV adverts could be used at the cost of £20 000 for a national campaign but this would take up most of the company's budget.
- Henderson's Toys could attend trade fairs and collectors' fairs to raise their profile and generate sales.

Place

- Henderson's Toys could sell over the internet using their own website.
- They could also use internet retailers such as Amazon and eBay to sell their products.
- They could also use local stores in Harrogate, Leeds, York etc. to distribute their product, extending this to stores such as Hamleys in the future.
- Henderson's Toys should extend their market to the international market using mail order through the internet. This would have an additional cost of package and postage for the company. They could, however, arrange a contract with a distribution company with a 'bulk buying' contract.
- E-commerce could be used alongside traditional 'bricks and mortar' retailers.
- Cheaper suppliers could be sought with better 'bulk buying' contracts.

Extended marketing mix

- People – Henderson's Toys could consider employing a marketing manager with experience in e-commerce. They will also need to employ a logistics/distribution manager to manage the process of packaging and postage.
- Physical environment – Henderson's Toys should ensure that all the outlets they use are high-quality, upmarket retailers to match the brand image. They could also consider running tours of the factory and create a museum housing their toys through history.
- Process – They need to develop an effective and efficient way of managing their e-commerce and 'bricks and mortar' orders. This could be done by using a database.

Budget

Newspaper advert – fortnightly for 12 months	£15 600
Website design and upkeep	£798
Magazine adverts	£10 400
TV advert	£20 000

Total = £46 798

- £46 798 has been spent, including a TV advert, which may not be cost effective.
- £28 202 has been left over for a contingency budget and to provide funds for contracts with online retailers and the cost of trade fairs.

Timescale

- The plan has been put together for 12 months as Henderson's Toys need to make sure that this marketing campaign works effectively in raising more sales revenue.
- During the marketing campaign each medium used should be evaluated and at the end of 12 months Henderson's Toys could continue with the ones which have been the most successful.

Evaluation

Henderson's Toys will know whether their marketing campaign is successful by comparing the performance of the business against their marketing objectives:

- To re-establish Henderson's Toys as a high-quality luxury toy provider within 12 months
- To increase brand awareness of Henderson's Toys across the UK and internationally within 12 months
- To establish the brand within the adult collectors' market within two years
- To increase sales revenue to £2 million within three years

Unit 3: Personal and Business Finance

Revision test 1 (pages 45–63)

1 Possible answers: Unit of account, means of exchange, store of value, legal tender

2 A pawnbroker lends money against the value of a person's assets, e.g. jewellery. They then charge interest on the loan for the period during which the money is borrowed. Suggested answer: If the pawned items are not bought back within a certain time they may be sold by the pawnbroker to recover the debt.

3 Answers may include the following points, for example:

(i) When the Bank of England raises interest rates, the cost of borrowing will rise. It will become more expensive to borrow money. Borrowers will be affected because their monthly repayments on loans or mortgages will increase. Some borrowers may find it difficult to finance the increased cost of borrowing.

(ii) Faced by higher borrowing costs, borrowers may have fewer funds for other expenses. They might fall into arrears with bills and paying back loans. In extreme circumstances, if a borrower is unable to pay, their goods or property may be repossessed.

4 Answers may include the following points, for example: For personal customers, the use of the latest banking technologies offers convenience, greater control of their bank account and finances, quick access to balances and fewer visits to bank branches as customers have instant access to a range of banking services 24 hours a day, seven days a week, whether at home or on the move. Telephone banking allows customers to carry out automated transactions. Customers can also access other services, such as setting up standing orders, and there is also the option to talk directly to a member of staff. Online banking allows customers to check and manage their account. Customers can make payments online, on the phone or in a branch in less than two hours. Customers may be able to apply for bank loans and mortgages online and have access to customer service staff to answer queries. The latest mobile apps give users access to a wide range of banking services.

For business customers, electronic banking has many advantages. Balances can be checked instantly and funds can be transferred easily between accounts. Suppliers can be paid electronically and payments for invoices received electronically, reducing the time traditionally taken by cheques for payment. In addition, electronic banking can work alongside the business's accounting software. Electronic payments have significantly reduced the time required to transfer funds from one bank account to another. BACs, which takes three working days is

used to transfer payment from one account to another, and is mainly used by organisations for direct debits and credits. CHAPs usually guarantees payment to be made on the same day.
The main disadvantages include possible breaches of security, banking fraud, and forgetting security log-ins and passwords. The ease with which customers can access their accounts may encourage overspending.

5 Answers may include the following points, for example: An ISA is an Individual Savings Account which does not charge individuals tax on the interest earned on their savings, unlike other deposit or savings accounts where tax is payable on the interest.
There are two types: the cash and the stocks and shares ISA. Some ISAs are instant access. Medium-term ISAs tie up the funds for one to five years in return for a higher rate of interest. Each person has a tax-free limit each year.
ISAs are seen as tax-efficient ways of saving. Unlike a pension, an ISA allows you to access the funds when they are needed. There is a wide range of different ISAs to suit most people and their circumstances. They enable people to build up funds to create a lump sum for the future.
BUT:
It depends on what kind of ISA is being bought. Cash ISAs are safer, but the returns are much lower. An ISA based on shares can earn more interest but the value of shares can go down as well as up. ISAs can also be seen as a long-term investment. This means that they are ideal for someone that is happy to lock their money into the investment for a longer period of time. There can also be significant management charges from financial institutions to look after the investment for the customer.
On balance an assessment would be that there are ISAs to match the needs of most investors, they are tax efficient, but unless risks are taken, the return on the investment is modest.

6 Answers may include the following points, for example:
- Stockbridge Insurance offers the cheapest annual premium (£1250) with Cranford Insurance quoting the highest premium (£1844). However, Eleni needs to take into account the other features included or on offer with each of the policies.
- Eleni can pay for her insurance in instalments with three of the companies but only Rutland Cars does not charge extra for paying in instalments (12 x £120 = £1440 which is the same cost as the annual premium). United Insurers offers instalments but Eleni would have to pay £1440 for the insurance – the same cost for the insurance policy as Rutland Cars.
- The compulsory excess is the amount of any claim that would need to be met by Eleni in addition to the voluntary excess she has opted to pay. For the cheapest insurance (Stockbridge), the compulsory excess is £700 which means that, if Eleni claimed on this policy, she would have to pay £1200 towards the cost of the claim.
- Windscreen cover is included in all the policies but only Cranford, the most expensive policy, does not include an excess.
- All the policies include breakdown cover, with Carterton plc providing the cheapest cover at £35 per month.
- Eleni uses her car for work and travels in excess of 1000 miles per month. She needs to decide if she can afford to pay the annual premium in full or if she wishes to pay in monthly instalments. If she does not have sufficient funds to pay the full annual premium, then Rutland Cars may be her best choice since it does not charge a fee for paying in instalments and has lower excesses for both windscreen cover and a courtesy car compared with United Insurers. She may decide that the additional £42 in monthly payments for the Cranford Insurance policy is too expensive even though it does not include any excess on windscreen insurance and provides a free courtesy car.
  Although the monthly payments on the United Insurers policy is also £120 (the same as Rutland Cars), it has a higher excess and additional costs for the courtesy car than Rutland Cars.
  Should Eleni wish to pay the annual premium in full, then Carterton plc may offer the best value given that it has a lower voluntary excess than both Stockbridge Insurance and United Insurers; a courtesy car is included free of charge and breakdown cover is the lowest of all the policies.

7 Possible answers: Wages paid to the players and full-time employees; inventory (stock); rent; rates; heating and lighting; water; insurance; administration and administrative costs (telephone, postage, stationery and printing); wages and salaries paid to players and full-time employees; marketing; bank charges; interest paid on loans and mortgages; straight-line depreciation; reducing-balance depreciation; discounts to customers.

8 Answers may include the following points: Intangible assets These are non-physical capital items that the business plans to use over a long period of time. They include goodwill, patents, trademarks and brand names. The football club will sell branded goods, such as scarves and replica shirts.

9 (a) $\frac{996}{4} = 249$
$996 - 249 = 747$
$747 \times £13 = £9711$
$249 \times £7 = £1743$
$£9711 + £1743 = £11\,454$

(b) $23 \times £11{,}454 = £263\,442$
$\frac{1240}{4} = 310$
$1240 - 310 = 930$
Therefore:
$930 \times £13 = £12\,090$
$310 \times £7 = £2170$
$£12\,090 + £2170 = £14\,260$
$£14\,260 \times 6 = £85\,560$
$£263\,442 + £85\,560 = £349\,002$

(c) Lamb $= \frac{600}{900} = 67$p
Beef $= \frac{700}{1200} = 58$p
Chicken $= \frac{480}{700} = 69$p
Vegetarian $= \frac{500}{700} = 71$p (biggest contribution per unit)

(d) $67 + 58 + 69 + 71 = \frac{£265}{4} = 66$p average contribution
The best contribution is offered by the vegetarian pie, but fewer of these are sold than beef and lamb.

10 (a) Total costs = £12 000 + (£4 × 8000) = £44 000
Total income = £8 × 8000 = £64 000
Therefore:
£64 000 – £44 000 = £20 000 profit

(b) Fixed costs = £12 000
Variable costs = £4 per unit
Revenue per unit = £8
Therefore:
Contribution per unit = £8 – £4 = £4
Break-even point $= \frac{£12\,000}{£4} = 3000$
3000 units need to be sold for the print shop to break even.

11 Answers may include the following points, for example: Without necessarily knowing whether the club is profitable or not, the choices may be comparatively limited. In this case the club may have to rely on the support of one or more wealthy supporters or the more general financial support from fans. With a good fan base, Howard could consider crowd-funding or donations. He could take out a loan secured against assets, or perhaps a mortgage secured against the ground itself. Howard needs to raise £35 000. If he has sufficient personal funds himself he could choose to put in his own capital to fund the shortfall (owner's capital).

12 Answers may include the following points, for example: The statement of comprehensive income sets out the business's revenue and expenses. In the case of the purchase of the coach, the club needs to budget for additional expenses such

as fuel, maintenance and other running costs. This will have a negative impact on any profits or surpluses generated from operating the coach. However, the increase in expenses will, in part, be offset by the additional income generated from the hire contract with the local sports club. The football club should plan to at least cover its additional expenses. Non-current assets, such as the coach, lose their value over time and are therefore subject to depreciation. The value of this depreciation is shown in the statement of comprehensive income.

The club's statement of financial position records what the club is owed (its assets) and owes (its liabilities). The coach represents a non-current asset and since the club has used some of its cash reserves to pay for it (rather than take out a loan), its current assets are reduced while liabilities remain the same. Since non-current assets lose their value over time, the value of the coach shown in the statement of financial position is reduced in successive years based upon the value of depreciation that has been calculated by the straight-line method. The following calculation shows the amount of depreciation shown in the statement of comprehensive income and the value of the coach that will be recorded in the statement of financial position over the four-year period.

Straight-line method for calculating annual depreciation:

$$\frac{(£8000 - £500)}{4} = \frac{£7500}{4} = £1875$$

£1875 will therefore be included in the profit or loss account in the statement of comprehensive income to denote the annual depreciation of the coach.

	£
	8000
Depreciation: Year 1	(1875)
	6125
Depreciation: Year 2	(1875)
	4250
Depreciation: Year 3	(1875)
	2375
Depreciation: Year 4	(1875)
Disposal value	500

13 Answers may include the following points, for example:
Venture capital aims to provide a source of long-term and committed capital aimed at encouraging a business to grow. It provides financial backing while not taking away the day-to-day control of the business from the original owners. Lenders have a legal right to be paid interest and to receive the capital back, but they are more interested in the growth and profitability of the business as this increases the value of their investment in the business.

Owners will have to be prepared to lose part of their stake in the business to the venture capital company and it might mean that a non-executive director takes a place on the board. This expertise can be very valuable to the business.

In addition to the finance, the venture capital company can offer guidance and help with a variety of decisions. They can also provide services such as legal and tax support to the business. The venture capital company also has good contacts in the business community that it can use to the advantage of the business.

The downside mainly focuses on loss of control. The size of the venture capital company's stake will determine just how much control they demand. If they own more that 50% then the original owners have effectively lost control of their business.

The key questions to ask are:

- Would the owners prefer a smaller business that they wholly own or a smaller share of a much larger business?
- Do they want to have input from external experts to help them in the future?
- Could the business profit from having access to contacts and support that a venture capital company can offer?

Ultimately, the club's chances of being able to attract such funding depends on whether a venture capital company sees potential growth and profit in the future. They also want to see skilled and ambitious management. If these are in place then the club has a good chance of being able to attract a venture capital company.

14 Answers may include the following points, for example:
Profitability has dropped slightly. The gross profit margin last year stood at 44% and now it is 41%. There could be very straightforward reasons for this. The underlying net profit margin has not moved very much (13% down to 12%). This is a better indication of the overall profit performance of the business.

ROCE has increased, so there is a slight increase in return on investment. This should be seen as positive for investors.

Current ratio is marginal; the shop can just about cover their short-term liabilities. The situation this current year to last year has improved slightly. The shop is perfectly capable of covering its financial commitments.

Liquid capital ratio – this has slightly improved but is still below the recommended minimum. The figure has barely changed, but the business should try to improve this situation.

Trade receivables are taking slightly longer to pay, which is not good. Trade payables are shorter. This means that the shop has to pay suppliers quicker than they receive money from their creditors. Combined, this means that the shop is not performing well in this respect. They need to either collect the debts from customers quicker or delay the payment to suppliers. Failure to do this will affect the amount of working capital available to the business.

Overall the performance is slightly worse than last year.

Revision test 2 (pages 64–76)

1 Possible answers:
- The UK's central bank – regulates and supervises banks, building societies, insurance companies, investment companies and credit unions
- Responsible for maintaining the UK's monetary and financial stability
- Sets interest rates – if Bank increases rates, the cost of borrowing will rise
- Issues legal tender

2 Possible answers may include the first point plus two others:
- Financial cooperatives owned and run by their members
- Not-for-profit organisations
- Offers members savings accounts, current accounts and loans
- More limited funds and opportunities than commercial banks and building societies
- Usually no service charge or minimum balances

3 Answers may include the following points, for example:
- Options and flexibility for customers – customers visit the bank to carry out transactions either over the counter or using automated self-service machines.
- Selling or providing other services – customers may also seek advice on financial services and products. Branch staff may try to sell additional products to customers who visit.
- Alternatives to online services – access is limited to branch opening hours, and customers may have to travel to get there, but the full range of services is offered.
- Personal services – branches provide customers with face-to-face contact with the bank, but the opening hours are limited.

4 Answers may include the following points, for example:
Regardless of changes in the interest rate, a fixed rate mortgage means that repayments are fixed for the duration of a set deal which can be one, two, three, five or ten years. It does mean that the couple will know exactly what their mortgage will cost. The repayments are fixed for the duration of the deal, which allows them to budget. However, the start rate is usually higher than variable rates. There are also penalties if the couple want to get out of the mortgage before the fix is over.

A tracker mortgage is variable. It uses an economic indicator such as the Bank of England base rate. The tracker will move in line with the indicator, up or down. Trackers are popular if there is a low interest rate or the interest rate is dropping. It will only change if the indicator changes. If the indicator rate rises then the tracker rate will go up. It is a fixed relationship, so the rate could increase by a large amount if the indicator goes up significantly.

5 Answers may include the following points, for example:
An IFA is an independent financial adviser (IFA). These are professional individuals who give independent advice and guidance on a range of financial products, e.g. mortgages, pensions and investments. Financial advisers are regulated by the Financial Conduct Authority. Consumers pay a fee for the advice.
An IFA is not tied financially to any single provider and can provide advice based on the whole of the market. In other words, they are in a position to identify, match and suggest the best options for their client.
An IFA has a legal obligation to provide their clients with the best advice. They will match the personal circumstances of the client and find the best option. They are obliged to provide their clients with reasons why they are offering particular advice.
An IFA as an expert and specialist in the area of work will constantly look for the best deals that are being offered.
Using their knowledge they will be able to assess whether an attractive deal would suit the needs of the client. They will also be in a position to be able to access the deal for their client.
Financial advisers that work for banks or other financial institutions are restricted in terms of what they can offer as they are obliged to suggest an option from a limited range offered by the financial institution. An IFA is obliged to do the opposite and search the whole market for the best matched deal.
All IFAs are regulated by the Financial Conduct Authority (FCA). This means that they must have relevant qualifications and be competent at their job. They must also show integrity and a professional approach.
Generally, an IFA can be used to save the client time, money and effort. They are able to make an objective judgement of the financial situation, follow the preferences and the objectives of the client and then match an ideal financial package. Although an IFA charges a fee for their work, this should be more than offset by the money and time that they save the client.

6 Answers may include the following points, for example:

Table 1: Payday loans information

APR	Monthly repayment	Terms (months)	Total payment due
1081%	£148.02	3	£444.06
1286.9%	£101.63	5	£508.15
1217%	£151.78	3	£455.34
1188%	£235.28	2	£470.56
1717%	£161.04	3	£483.12

The first option offers the lowest overall cost for the loan. However, it is important to note that this is £46.39 per month more than the lowest monthly payment plan. This could mean that Jenna might struggle to meet these payments. Consequently, it might be the case that she should go for Provider B as this is a lower monthly payment spread out over five months.

7 Answers may include two of the following points, for example:
- Cash sales – through over-the-counter transactions
- Credit sales – through sales using a method of credit
- Rent received – when a business rents out a property it owns
- Commission received – when a business acts as an agent for another business and receives a percentage of every sale
- Interest received – money earned on savings or lending
- Discount received – when a business pays a reduced price for goods or services

8 Answers may include the following points, for example:
The key advantages include:
- New investors bringing new skills and contacts into the business
- The fact that the funds mean that the business does not have to obtain a loan or pay interest on the borrowing
- The financial risk is shared with others

9 (a) The marketing budget was £40 000 but 20% overspent. Purchasing was £124 000, but 15% overspent. Sales budget was £490 000 but 20% up. Overheads, employees and other costs were budgeted at £88 000 but were 10% overspent. This can be seen more clearly in a table:

	Budget	Actual
Marketing	£40 000	£48 000
Purchasing	£124 000	£142 600
Sales	£490 000	£588 000
Overheads etc.	£88 000	£96 800
Totals	£490 000 – £252 000 = £238 000	£588 000 – £287 400 = £300 600

The budget shows a £238 000 difference between income and expenditure. The actual figures, despite the overspending, are more than offset by the increase in income. There is therefore a positive difference of £62 600 between the budgeted and actual figures.

(b) The total actual profit is £300 600. Therefore, a 10% share would be worth £30 060. Sonal has a 30% stake in the business. His share of the profit would be £90 180.

(c) At 500 units: $\frac{30\,000}{500} = £60$

At 4000 units: $\frac{108\,000}{4000} = £27.00$

The difference is therefore
£60 – £27.00 = £33.00

(d) At 4000 total revenue:
Total revenue 4000 × £99.99 = £399 960
Total cost @ 4000 = £108 000
Therefore £399 960 – £108 000 = £291 960

10 (a)

	Ring	Ball & Hoop	Puzzle	Snake
Selling price per unit	£2	£3	£2.50	£3.50
Labour costs	40p	45p	40p	40p
Material costs	20p	55p	30p	50p
Units sold	9000	12 000	6000	4000

Ring: £2 – 60p = £1.40; £1.40 × 9000 = £12 600
Ball and hoop: £3 – £1 = £2; £2 × 12 000 = £24 000
Puzzle: £2.50 – £0.70 = £1.80; £1.80 × 6000 = £10 800
Snake: £3.50 – £0.90 = £2.60; £2.60 × 4000 = £10 400
The ball and hoop product line provides the highest contribution.

(b) The total contribution provided by the four product lines = £57 800
Therefore £57 800 – £22,000 = £35 800

11 Answers may include the following points, for example:
It is usually the case that production levels are budgeted estimates of potential demand based on experience or previous sales figures. There are three possible scenarios:
- Sales are equal to production levels – this is extremely rare and unlikely. Few businesses have the ability to be able to correctly predict the precise sales for products into the future and to ensure that product exactly matches the figures.

- Sales are greater than production levels – this leaves the business with a shortfall in stock to sell to their customers. It means that customers are let down as there is no stock to supply them with or that they will have to wait for the stock to be manufactured for them. In either case this means placing the relationship between the customer and the business under strain.
- Sales are lower than production levels – this means that there is overproduction and the business is left with stock that it has not sold. All customers have been supplied, but the business has assets tied up in stock that cannot be sold at this time.

The implications for break-even are:

- Break-even assumes an ideal situation where sales match or exceed the total costs of the business and therefore produce a profit.
- However, it might not take into account that the business cannot produce more products over a given period of time to take advantage of the extra sales.
- If sales are greater and the business is able to produce additional stock then this does mean that the business will create a bigger profit. The break-even point is not affected.
- Break-even is supply side related only as it only considers the cost of sales.

12 Answers may include the following points, for example:
Oak Toys has a website. The owners have prepared their budgeted and actual profit figures for the e-business.

	1st quarter	2nd quarter	3rd quarter	4th quarter
	Budget/ Actual	**Budget/ Actual**	**Budget/ Actual**	**Budget/ Actual**
Profit	£3000/ (£8000)	£7000/ £8000	£9000/ £7000	£30 000/ £35 000

It is important for the business to measure the actual results against the budgeted figures. This is an essential part of evaluating the performance of the business. Where there is a difference this is known as a variance. Variances can either be favourable (better than expected) or unfavourable (worse than predicted). In this case, the first quarter loss and the disappointing third quarter profit are both unfavourable variances. The second quarter profit and the better fourth quarter results are examples of favourable variances.
The key purpose of the variance analysis is to try to work out what caused the difference between the actual and budgeted figures. The usual reasons for unfavourable variances are unrealistic budgets or poor performance (or budgetary control).
In terms of action, the business can:

- be better informed about the current business operations by considering the variances and the reasons behind them
- identify areas that have performed well or not so well and take corrective action
- ensure that they monitor, evaluate and control the areas of concern
- adjust the budgets up or down to be a better reflection of the real situation
- implement cost cutting where necessary
- focus on sales generation where necessary.

13 Answers may include the following points, for example:
Toy sales are seasonal. The low figures for the first quarter and the modest figures for the second and third quarters indicate that sales are very much focused on the last three months of the year. Many retailers see this pattern of sales and launch sales and other promotions throughout the year in order to stimulate sales.
Sales figures are rarely constant throughout the year. A business with seasonal products and services must try to maximise their sales at the points in the year where there is high demand. This is necessary as it means that these sales have to be sufficient in order to ensure that the business has sufficient funds to see them over periods when sales are very low.
In this case there is a major seasonal effect. This is a systematic and calendar-related effect shown in the sharp increase in sales leading up to the Christmas period. A business will usually try to make some seasonal adjustments in order to estimate and then to eliminate the huge change and reveal the underlying sales trends. It is actually the non-seasonal characteristics that are of most interest to the business.

14 Answers may include the following points, for example:
Oak Toys are always looking for ways to improve their profit margins. One of their key sellers is the puzzle pencil case. Normally it sells for £7.99 and the business sells 12 000 of them each year. They want to increase the price to £8.99 but think that sales will fall to 8000.
12 000 sales @ £7.99 = £95 880
8000 sales @ £8.99 = £71 920
The key points to cover include:

- Reduction in the turnover of the business by nearly £25 000
- Higher profit margin per unit, but the contribution required per unit will be higher
- Reduced ability of the business to be able to cover their fixed costs

Unit 6: Principles of Management

Revision task 1 (pages 78–99)

Revision activity 1

Below is an example of a formal report on the management challenges facing Brigstone Kitchens. Other approaches are possible.

Formal report on the current management challenges facing Brigstone Kitchens Ltd and suggested management actions
Recommendations for discussion
This report has been compiled by A. Learner and is intended for the Finance Director

Date: 16 June 2017

1. **Introduction**

1.1 The purpose of this report is to:

(i) propose a set of new strategic priorities
(ii) analyse the impact of the current management challenges faced by Brigstone Kitchens Ltd
(iii) propose a set of actions and recommendations that will address these challenges
(iv) recommend a Management Implementation Plan for moving the company forward.

2. **Proposed key strategic objectives**

2.1 The business is currently facing significant changes to its management team with both the Director of Operations and the Director of Finance likely to take on additional management responsibilities when the owner of the company relinquishes her current operational management duties.

2.2 This significant change in management responsibilities presents the company with the opportunity to establish a set of new strategic objectives which will prepare the company for the next stage in its development.

2.3 The proposed strategic priorities are as follows:

(i) Growth
(ii) Efficiency savings
(iii) Increasing productivity
(iv) The introduction of new products
(v) Introducing direct sales to the general public

2.4 Should these priorities be supported by the management of the company then a set of strategic objectives can be established which will provide the basis for setting challenging company targets which will impact positively upon the future business performance of the company.

3. **Current management challenges faced by Brigstone Kitchens Ltd**

3.1 An analysis of the three data tables that accompany this report highlight a number of challenges which must be addressed by management:

(i) The current profile of the total workforce (Table 1) shows that it is predominantly male (66%) with this figure increasing to 77.7% in the combined craft, assembly and finishing sections. The age profile in these three sections is 50 years or above with the average age in the craft section rising to 57 years. The challenges which must be addressed by management focus upon the future recruitment of highly skilled craft workers, the upskilling of the current work force, motivation and the willingness or otherwise of the workforce to accept changes in business practices.

(ii) The Director of Operations has taken the lead in increasing sales turnover over the last five years with turnover increasing from £2 400 000 in 2012 to £2 644 200 in 2016, resulting in an increase in gross profits from £1 400 00 to £1 489 200 over the same period. However these figures must be seen in the context of gross and net profit margins which over the same five-year period have both fallen – gross profit from 58% to 56% and, more alarmingly, net profit from 18% in 2012 to 12% in 2016. The fall in net profit is accounted for by an increase in operational costs and these must be subject to strict controls if the fall in profit margins is to be halted.

(iii) Productivity has fallen by 8.75% over the period 2012–2016 (400 units per annum per employee in 2012 to 365 units in 2016) whilst average salary has increased by over 8% (£18 500 in 2012 to £20 000 in 2016).

3.2 The management style adopted by the company's management team has resulted in low staff turnover. Employees respect the owner of the company, have significant autonomy in operational matters and are self-managed. There are few policies and procedures which results in a 'can do' attitude. These elements of a laissez-faire approach to management can bring significant benefits but can also result in difficulties, particularly if things start to go wrong since the levels of responsibility and accountability may be difficult to identify without a formal organisation chart and reporting structure.

3.3 The prevailing business culture – 'how things are done around here' – means that it is difficult to implement any significant changes to organisational practices apart from in specific sections of the workforce when personnel changes occur resulting in the recruitment of new employees. For example, in the Finance Section a new Business Support Manager has been appointed which, along with the installation of the new accounting software, will make it easier to set and monitor budgets and identify potential efficiency savings.
However, given the prevailing business culture, it is more difficult to implement changes which impact upon the whole of the company. The resistance to the proposed new wages scheme is an example of such resistance.

3.4 The lack of an identified management hierarchy and structure in the form of an organisation chart means that introducing policies and procedures for the management of physical and human resources is an additional challenge.

Policies and procedures need to be implemented and monitored with clear management reporting lines going up through the management hierarchy. As a result, any proposals for the introduction of individual performance targets within a Management by Objectives framework cannot be implemented since, at an operational level, there are no designated supervisors to take responsibility for agreeing the targets with individual employees and monitoring their progress.

3.5 There is also an issue of employee motivation in the company. A contented workforce may not always be a motivated workforce so that simply keeping the workers happy instead of motivating them does not motivate them to improve performance. Management motivational theory, such as Herzberg's two-factor theory of hygiene and motivational factors, identifies that if a business wants to motivate its employees then it must incorporate achievement, recognition and responsibility into its management practices. Clearly, the company's current management practices do not do this.

4. Proposals to address the current management issues

4.1 Establish a clear vision for the company, agreed by senior managers who will be responsible for communicating this vision to the workforce.

4.2 Engage in on-going discussions with the workforce to stress the urgency of the need for change centred upon the company's five-year trends in performance.

4.3 Produce a new draft organisation chart which introduces the role of Section Supervisor. As the first stage in this process, the Business Support Services Manager would take on line management responsibility for a newly created Division of Business Support Services which will integrate the staff currently working in finance, sales and design. In addition two new divisions will be created – Production and Direct Sales.

4.4 Respond to the current workforce concerns by establishing a wage scheme which retains the current system (although this will be based upon the company's ability to pay) and introduce a new component based upon the achievement of individual targets, agreed between individual workers and their supervisors, linked to the company's strategic objectives.

4.5 Establish a formal set of management policies and procedures to ensure that the new pay scheme is operated uniformly across the company.

4.6 Undertake a training needs analysis to identify the training needs of the new supervisors and implement a training programme to address any skill gaps identified.

4.7 Engage an external management consultant to work with senior managers on how to manage strategic change

5. Recommendations

5.1 It is recommended that a Management Implementation Plan is devised comprising the following elements:

(i) Senior managers agree a new set of strategic objectives based upon the strategic priorities identified in this report.

(ii) The owner takes responsibility for formulating a communications strategy focused upon workforce engagement.

(iii) The owner and senior managers design a new pay scheme based upon performance targets in each of the Divisions and these form the basis of targets for individual employees established within a new performance appraisal scheme.

(iv) The Director of Finance and the Director of Operations work together to:

- formulate a company organisation chart and prioritise the company policies and management processes required to implement and monitor the introduction of the new management systems
- produce a business plan for the establishment of a new Department of Business Support Systems and a Direct Sales Division. The plan can also be presented to financial institutions should the company require additional finance to support its long-term growth.

(v) The Director of Finance is responsible for costing all the proposals in the Management Implementation Plan including the introduction of supervisors, the training budget and the financial implications of the company's new business plan.

Revision activity 2

Below is an example of a set of presentation slides and speaker notes on the management challenges facing Brigstone Kitchens. Other approaches are possible.

Slide 1

1. Brigstone Kitchens Ltd

Improving management effectiveness and business performance

- Strategic priorities – identifying the way forward
- Business performance and the need for change
- Current management challenges
- Company performance
- Improvement plan
- Management Implementation Plan

Slide 1 speaker notes

- Introduce the presentation – context of the introduction of the new pay scheme
- Rationale – to address current company issues
- Introduction of the pay scheme needs to be seen in the context of wider issues to be covered in the presentation

Slide 2

2. Key strategic priorities

- Growth
- Efficiency savings
- Increased productivity
- Introduction of new products
- Introducing direct sales to the public

Slide 2 speaker notes

- Growth – new products; new markets; opportunities to improve profitability (gross and net profit margins); attract new investors
- Efficiency savings – lower production costs and expenses
- Increased productivity – organise workforce so that employees are clearly focused upon targets
- New products – opportunities for increased investment; new markets; reduced business risks
- Direct sales to the public – linked to business growth and profitability; potential for more investors to come on board

Slide 3

3. Current management challenges

Management challenge	Impact on the business
Workforce profile	Motivation to take on new responsibilities Potential recruitment difficulties
Management	No defined structure Management responsibilities are unclear
Business performance	Inefficiencies Higher costs Lower productivity

Slide 3 speaker notes

- Impact of workforce profile – composition; motivation; recruitment
- Management – the need for structure to promote target-setting and confirm management responsibilities at all levels in the business; promote change
- Business performance – get a clearer understanding of business performance; profit margins; productivity

Slide 4

4. Business performance

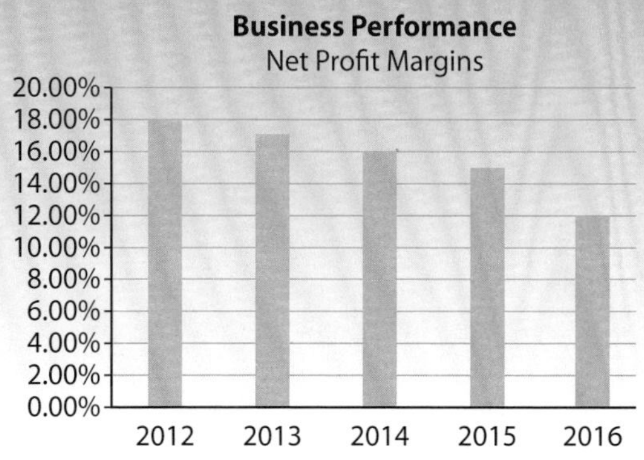

Slide 4 speaker notes

- Increase in sales turnover (positive) – commend Peter's effort
- Increase in year-on-year sales turnover and gross profits

BUT

- Net profit has DECREASED year-on-year for the last five years
- Net profit margins REDUCED from 18% (2012) to 12% (2016)

Slide 5

5. Management proposals

Proposal	Rationale
Agree strategic objectives	To determine the long-term direction of the business
Communication strategy	To share the vision with the workforce
New organisation chart	To create the new departments
New wage scheme	To increase productivity
Update policies and procedures	To streamline operations

Slide 5 speaker notes

- Agree strategic objectives: strategy is concerned with the long term; stress the urgency of the change (performance); identify the risks if the company doesn't change
- Need for a clear business plan if we need to raise additional capital to finance the proposed new developments
- Engage with employees – call a meeting/work with individuals (influencers/leaders)
- Identify win-win scenarios for managers and employees – performance bonuses
- Create winners in the workforce – supervisor role
- Communicate and celebrate gains (confirm the vision)
- Implement new policies and procedures
- Embed the procedures into the 'fabric' of company management

PLUS

- Stress the need for training – including senior managers (specialist management consultant could be engaged to work with senior managers to identify appropriate change management strategies)

Slide 6

6. Recommendations

WHAT?	WHY?	WHO?
Agree strategic objectives	To establish long-term vision	Owner plus senior managers
Communications with the workforce	To establish 'workforce buy-in'	Owner
New pay scheme	Improve productivity	Directors
Organisation chart	New departments created	Directors
Business plan	Targets and finance	Directors
Costings	Promote efficiencies	Director of Finance

Slide 6 speaker notes

- Proposed strategic priorities → management challenges and impact → actions → recommendations
- Any questions or comments?
- Pose the following questions:
  - Can the company afford to stay as we are given the management challenges identified in this presentation?
  - Are there alternatives to what has been proposed in this presentation?

Revision task 2 (pages 100–111)

Revision activity 1

Your report could include the following points, for example:

1 Company performance
  - Although sales revenue increased by 17.4%, both the cost of sales and operating expenses rose by a greater percentage, leaving both gross profit and particularly operating profit significantly reduced.
  - The increase in employees from 14 000 to 18 500 (+32%) may have greatly affected the operating expenses.

2 Organisational structure
  - Possible scenarios include:
    - Combine together the two production departments
    - Quality assurance + customer services
    - Human resources + training and development
    - Sales and marketing + online sales
    - Create one retail division
    - Merge administration with IT services
    - Retain product design and research as a separate division or merge with production; may also be opportunities for cross-company matrix approach with a project team with members drawn from different divisions including production, sales and marketing and HR

3 Managing change
  - A reduction in the number of divisions may provide the scope for a more streamlined directorate.
  - Thought needs to be given in the report regarding the impact on those directors who 'lose out' in the restructuring programme, essentially redeployment or redundancy.
  - In any event careful consideration is required to ensure that the company (i) follows its own procedures and (ii) has regard to existing employment legislation (a detailed knowledge of legislation is not required).
  - The costs and benefits of the reorganisation should be articulated in the report, e.g. costs of potential redundancy and benefits of streamlined and effective management team.
  - At the supervisory level there is similar scope for rationalisation. New job roles could be created at the supervisory level in the management hierarchy.
  - An in-house training plan could be drawn up based upon a skills audit conducted on the new supervisory staff.
  - Due regard should again be given to potential for a reduction in the number of supervisors.
  - The strategy could be presented to the workforce as a management restructuring with any future changes to the composition and size of the workforce being dependent upon company performance.
  - Target-setting could be used as a focus for the new management and supervisory personnel, filtered down to team and individual performance targets.
  - Two immediate issues to address (in terms of targets) would be the issues relating to the online sales platform and the associated customer service problems.

4 Managing quality
  - The important factor to identify in this section would be the MD's preference for an accredited quality system which would seem to count against the introduction of a company-devised TQM system.
  - ISO standards would appear to be appropriate in that they provide internationally recognised quality kite marks and accreditation for a company's quality assurance framework e.g. ISO9001:2015 (a detailed knowledge of the standard is not required); Six Sigma is also appropriate as an accredited framework.
  - The new HR and training division could also be tasked with preparing managers and their staff for IIP accreditation.
  - The benefits of a formalised quality management system should be highlighted in the report. For example:
    - Zero defect production and output
    - Continuous improvement
    - Improved output quality
    - Customer involvement and retention
    - Improved efficiency and profitability

5 Recommendations
  - The report should identify a set of recommendations which are unambiguous, practical, relevant, appropriate and in line with the analysis put forward
  - The recommendations should focus upon:
    - a new organisational structure
    - communicating the rationale of the new structure to the workforce
    - a plan to deal with displaced managers and supervisors (depending upon the proposed new structure)
    - target-setting priorities
    - training needs analysis and an associated training programme
    - identifying an appropriate accredited quality management system

Revision activity 2

Your slides and speaker notes could include the following points, for example.

1 Slide 1 should introduce the main themes of the presentation.

2 There should be a slide (suggest Slide 2) which provides a high-level analysis of performance data; it would be useful if this slide included a chart or diagram showing the difference in performance over the two-year period.

3 The final slide (Slide 6) should list the recommendations.

4 Slides 3, 4 and 5 would then be free to cover:
  - the new organisational structure
  - the quality management framework
  - the rationale for the change (including costs and benefits)

5 Good practice points which would improve the answer include:
  - the visual impact of the presentation (graphs, tables and process charts)
  - the quality of the speaker notes provided:
    - amplify the points made in each slide
    - in note format and not continuous prose

Unit 7: Business Decision Making

Revision task 1 (pages 113–128)

Revision activity 1

Individual responses. The report may be completed in individual ways, and different approaches to a formal report on Value Supermarkets are possible. The report below gives an alternative approach to the guided report as a further example, which you can review against your own work.

Formal Report on Brunton proposal
Date: 16 June 2017
Recommendation for discussion
This report has been compiled by A. Learner and is intended for the Project Manager

1. Introduction

1.1 The purpose of this report is:
- (i) to present an analysis of the factors that may influence the decision of Value Supermarkets to locate in the UK town of Brunton
- (ii) to provide an overview of the current market for online grocery sales and identify the potential opportunities and business risks for Value Supermarkets of expanding into this area.

1.2 The financial targets associated with this proposal would be as follows:
- (i) annual sales turnover of £8.5 million
- (ii) 20% gross profit margin, generating a gross profit of £1.7 million
- (iii) 12% net profit margin of 12% generating a net profit of £1 020 000

2. Characteristics of Brunton

2.1 Brunton's town centre has a number of characteristics which would contribute towards Value Supermarkets' overall business strategy, including its corporate social responsibility objectives.

2.2 Brunton's town centre is not currently reaching its potential largely due to the quality of its existing stock of business premises which do not meet the needs of local businesses. However, the local Council has earmarked funds available to address this issue which will be used to redevelop the town centre.

2.3 Given Value Supermarkets' preference for refurbishing existing business premises, this would present potential opportunities to work in partnership with the Council and to secure additional finance which could offset some of the refurbishment costs which would otherwise be met by the business.

2.4 In common with a number of towns in the UK there is a local retail park in the area but this is subject to planning restrictions which will impact positively on the Council's aim to redevelop the town centre since any significant new business developments are likely to be based in the town centre resulting in an increase in trade and business activity.

2.5 Value Supermarkets would have access to a workforce comprising both high- and low-skilled workers. Although many of the higher skilled members of the workforce gain employment outside of Brunton, the development of the town centre would create additional employment opportunities for this section of the workforce who may be attracted by lower travel to work costs.

2.6 An analysis of the labour force (2014) identified that 8.1% of Brunton's workforce has no qualifications and that 11.0% of the workforce were in receipt of some form of welfare benefits. Value Supermarkets' corporate social responsibility strategy could be focused on creating employment and training opportunities for the significant proportion of the local workforce who have low levels of qualifications.

3. Population analysis

3.1 Figure 1 shows the percentage breakdown of Brunton's total population of 283 000.

Figure 1

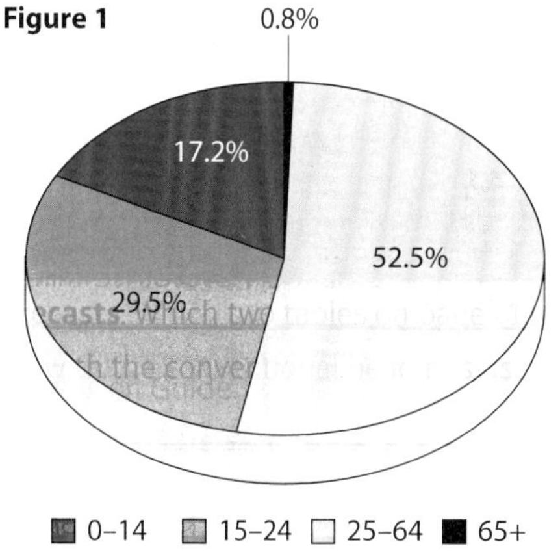

3.2 From Figure 1 it can be seen that the largest proportion of the population is in the 25–64 age group which accounts for nearly 150 000 people, with the 15–24 age group accounting for nearly 30% of the total population at almost 83 500 people. Less than 1% of the population is above 65 years of age. These figures would indicate that there would be a sufficient supply of labour to meet the demands of Value Supermarkets.

3.3 Average wage rates for those sections of the total population which make up the working population are below the UK national average. For example, in the 25–64 age group, average wage rates are 72% of the UK national average wage. This figure is likely to be influenced by the relatively high proportion of the workforce who have no qualifications or are in receipt of welfare benefits.

4. **Labour market analysis**

4.1 The latest figures show that 78.4% of the workforce are currently in work. Additional information is required to analyse the composition of the 21.6% of the workforce who are currently not in employment although it can be assumed that the relatively high proportion of the workforce without formal qualifications will exert a negative influence on the ability of this section of the working population to find suitable employment opportunities.

4.2 Figure 2 shows the percentage growth forecasts for occupations in Brunton over the period 2016–22.

Figure 2

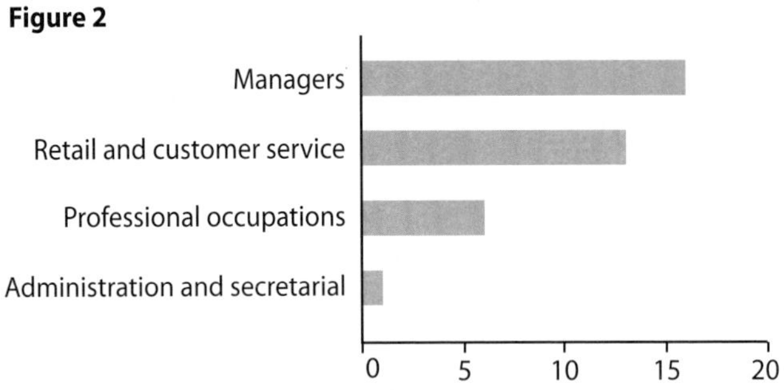

4.3 The impact of the Council's plans for the redevelopment of the town centre is reflected in the projected growth forecasts for occupations in Brunton over the period 2016–22 which identify a growth forecast of over 15% in managerial positions and a forecast growth of over 13% in retail and customer service occupations.

4.4 Figure 3 identifies the predicted changes in employment by sector in Brunton over the period 2016–22. The forecast increase in employment in the business services sector of over 35% is a significant factor to take into account given the importance of an efficient distribution system and the IT infrastructure which would be required by Value Supermarkets should it venture into online grocery sales.

Figure 3

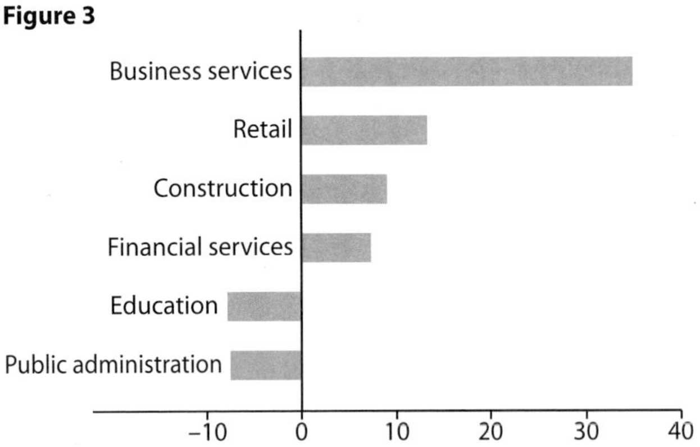

4.5 The projected increase in employment in the construction sector of just over 9% is a sign of increasing business activity in the area which may exert a positive influence on the level of consumer demand.

4.6 The projected fall in employment in public administration and education may be influenced by reductions in government expenditure brought about by government policies to reduce the size of the public sector deficit.

5. **Competitor analysis**

5.1 The competitor analysis in this report is based on the available data of a major supermarket, Bestco plc, which is based in the Brunton Retail Park and located six miles from the town centre. Further analysis would need to be undertaken of the composition of retail outlets in the Brunton town centre.

5.2 The Bestco plc supermarket offers a diversified range of both grocery and non-grocery items, including clothing, electronics and consumer electrical goods. It also has an in-store café. The diversified product range provides the opportunity to increase the average spend per customer.

5.3 8% of its total sales in its current product range is generated from its low-cost range of groceries which compete directly with the current product range of Value Supermarkets.

5.4 Bestco plc is a leading UK supermarket accounting for 28% of market share. However, its market share has reduced by 4 percentage points over the last five years which would indicate that it is losing ground to its competitors.

5.5 Further weaknesses in the overall business profile of Bestco plc compared with Value Supermarkets relate to performance indicators for customer retention and inventory turnover. Value Supermarkets has a higher customer retention than Bestco plc (80% compared to 65%). Customer retention is an important performance indicator for Value Supermarkets given its target financial performance indicators which, on a target annual sales turnover of £8.5 million, require an average monthly sales turnover of £708 333 per month.

5.6 Value Supermarkets also secure greater efficiencies in inventory turnover which can result in significant cost savings. Efficiency savings will impact upon Value Supermarkets' gross profit margin of 20%, which on a projected sales turnover of £8.5 million amounts to £1.7 million per year.

6. **Risk analysis**

6.1 There are two major risks of locating in Brunton. The first is the existence of an established major competitor who is able to offer a diversified product range of both grocery and non-grocery products. Although its market share is under pressure, it is still likely to retain a significant measure of customer loyalty.

6.2 Secondly the challenge of recruiting and training the workforce will centre upon the current skill levels within the working population in which 11% are benefit claimants, many of whom may not possess formal qualifications. Recruitment of managerial and supervisory staff may also be a challenge since other businesses may be moving into the area who will also be recruiting this level of staff. There may be some upward pressure on local wage rates if this is the case.

7. **Opportunities and business risks – a summary**

7.1 There are significant opportunities for Value Supermarkets locating in Brunton which can be summarised as follows:

(i) Brunton town centre is being redeveloped.

(ii) There may be opportunities to obtain financial support from the Council to refurbish existing retail premises.

(iii) There are currently parts of the existing workforce who are economically inactive and could be recruited to work in the new store.

Revision activity 2

Individual responses. Here are examples of four presentation slides and speaker notes which summarise the report's findings on the proposed Brunton supermarket location and the online grocery shopping platform, against which you can review your own work. Other approaches are possible.

Slide 1

Brunton – profile

- Population 282,415
- No major supermarkets in town centre
- Brunton Retail Park – major local shopping area
- Poor quality of business property stock in town centre
- Ambitious plans for redevelopment of town centre
- Significant unemployment
- High mobility of working population with higher level qualifications

Slide 1 Speaker notes

- Town centre will be redeveloped (with financial aid)
- Planning restrictions to be imposed on developments in the retail park (Bestco plc is the main 'local' supermarket located in the retail park)
- 10% fall in unemployment over the last four years
- 78.4% of the working population are in employment
- Unemployment likely to be linked to lack of qualifications (8.1% of the working population have no formal qualifications)
- Additional data:
  - 11% benefit claimants in working population
  - Strong growth projections (2016–22) in the employment of managers (15.8%) and customer service staff (13.2%)

Slide 2

Competitor profile – Bestco plc

- The UK's leading supermarket
- 28% market share
- Diversified product range (grocery and non-grocery)
- 20% of sales generated from low-cost range groceries
- Market share falling over the last four years
- Customer retention and inventory turnover KPIs are both below that of Value Supermarkets

Slide 2 Speaker notes

- Located in Brunton Retail Park (6 miles from Brunton town centre)
- Product range of 1600 with 1000 traditional grocery items products generating 62% of total sales; low-cost range of 200 items generates 8% of total sales (Value Supermarkets low cost range: 1100 products generate 99.48% of total sales)
- –4% fall in market share over the last five years
- Customer retention 65% (Value Supermarkets 80%)
- Inventory turnover 8 (Value Supermarkets 10)

Slide 3

Risk analysis

Risk factor	Comments
Bestco plc is major competitor	Financial strength Established customer base Diversified product offer
Potential increase in the number of competitors	Redevelopment of the town centre will attract more businesses
Increase in labour costs	Competition between businesses could force up wage rates
Switch away from low-cost groceries	Increase in the standard of living due to employment opportunities and higher wages

Slide 3 Speaker notes

- Bestco plc has the financial muscle to engage in a price war with Value Supermarkets in order to retain its customer base, e.g. loss leaders; special offers; up-selling
- Bestco plc could also increase the range of its current low-cost products
- Businesses will be attracted by financial assistance provided by the local authority and better quality business premises (construction is projected to expand over the period 2016–22 with more workers being employed)
- Labour market forecasts over the period 2016–22 show increases of +12.6% in retail employment and +35.2% in business services
- There is likely to be a direct relationship between the standard of living and the % of household income spent on higher-priced products

Slide 4

Opportunities for Value Supermarkets in Brunton

- Competitive advantage
- Town centre redevelopment
- Consumer demand
- Labour market changes
- Contribution to the company's business strategy and values
- But what is the biggest risk of locating in Brunton?

Slide 4 Speaker notes

- Value Supermarkets' low-cost grocery range; KPIs (customer retention and inventory turnover); falling market share of Bestco plc
- Financial assistance will be given to businesses locating in the town centre
- Supply of qualified workers may increase over time; more people may choose to take up local jobs rather than travel to other towns to secure employment
- There are opportunities for the company to engage in local regeneration projects which engage with unemployed workers providing them with job opportunities and improving their standard of living

Revision task 2 (pages 129–137)

Revision activity 1

Individual responses. Below is an example of a business plan for Ashbury Construction presented in the style of a formal report, against which you can review your own work. Other approaches are possible.

Ashbury Construction Business Plan
Date: 16 June 2017
This report has been compiled by A. Learner and is intended for providers of business finance and potential investors

1. **Background**

1.1 Ashbury Construction is an established business that specialises in supplying tools and building materials to the construction industry. Its most recent income statement shows that the business made a gross profit of £120 000 with a net profit of £20 000. The company wishes to expand in order to take advantage of the business opportunities which will arise from the proposed construction of new housing developments in the local area. Business finance is required to purchase or lease capital equipment that the company will hire out to local construction firms.

2. **Analysis of Ashbury Construction financial statements**

2.1 Income Statement

2.1.1 Sales turnover for the most recent income statement was £200 000 which generated £120 000 gross profit. This shows a healthy gross profit margin of 60%. Business expenses totalled £100 000 resulting in a net profit of £20 000 generating a net profit margin of 10%.

2.2 Statement of Financial Position

2.2.1 The business is in a healthy position with assets totalling £88 000 of which £38 000 are fixed assets.

2.2.2 The business has sufficient working capital of £35 000 to meet its day-to-day business expenses. Although there is the potential for bad debts which may arise from the £20 000 currently owed to the business by its customers, the business has cash and bank deposits of £20 000 which will be sufficient to cover any such bad debts, even after taking into account the £10 000 inventory.

2.2.3 The Statement of Financial Position (SOFP) shows that the business currently owes £15 000 to its suppliers but it does not have any long-term liabilities in the form of business loans which means that it could take on additional long-term business finance in the form of a bank loan.

2.2.4 The return on capital investment (ROCE) is healthy giving the current owner a return on the £65 000 capital identified in the SOFP of over 30%.

3. **Projected cash flow forecast**

3.1 The cash flow forecast submitted with this business plan identifies the projected income and expenditure flows that will be generated over the next year.

3.2 The cash flow forecast is based upon the purchase of the *Titan 100* generator and the forecast rental income from this generator is shown separately at £2000 per month in the income section of the cash flow forecast. The loan repayments for the purchase of this equipment are shown as £1000 per month in the expenditure section of the cash flow forecast.

3.3 Total income from both sales and equipment rental is forecast to be £203 000 for the 12-month period covered by the cash flow forecast. This is a 1.5% increase in income over the previous year's trading income of £200 000.

3.4 Purchase of the generator will impact on the Statement of Financial Position; the generator will be identified as a non-current asset although this will be offset by the corresponding increase in non-current, long-term liabilities.

3.5 Overall the cash flow forecast is healthy. Income streams over the period covered by the forecast show that income reduces in the winter months due to the downturn in business activity in the construction sector. March and April show that expenditure exceeds income but the business has sufficient working capital to meet these shortfalls.

4. **Equipment costs and benefits**

4.1 The business plan and cash flow forecast are based upon the purchase of the *Titan 100* generator. The benefit of choosing this equipment is that the business will be able to hire it out to existing customers which will impact positively on cash flow. Moving forward, the business would aim to secure contracts with new customers involved in bigger construction projects that would require larger generators.

4.2 Over the five-year expected life of the *Titan 100* generator there would be an estimated cash inflow of £62 000 which, when the purchase price of £40 000 is taken into account, gives a net cash inflow of £22 000. The corresponding figure for the *Titan 500* generator would be £30 000 (£86 000 – £56 000).

4.3 The net present value (NPV) based upon a 5% rate of interest provides a significant NPV of £15 664 for the *Titan 100* generator as shown in the following table:

Year	Cash flow	Discount factor (5%)	Discounted cash flow
0			(£40 000)
1	24 000	0.952	£22 848
2	16 000	0.907	£14 512
3	10 000	0.860	£8600
4	8000	0.823	£6584
5	4000	0.780	£3120
		Net present value	£15 664

5. **Market analysis**

5.1 Planning permission has been given for the construction of 600 low-cost housing units in the local area and this will form the basis of the business's target market. Further opportunities will develop as a result of the resurgence of the construction industry.

6. **Risk analysis**

6.1 The following risks have been identified in the following areas:

(i) Financial risks
(ii) Legal risks
(iii) Reputational risks

6.2 The following table identifies the potential risks to the business of the three categories of business risks.

Business risk	Details	Impact
Financial	Planning permission refused for new housing development	Reduced sales turnover
	Downturn in the economy	Less demand for new houses resulting in reduced sales
	Bad debts from new contracts	Reduced working capital and cash flow
Legal	Injuries caused by equipment hired out to customers	Fines
	Contractual disputes with customers	Legal fees
Reputational	Equipment breakdown	Fewer customers

6.3 In order to manage these risks the business will put in place the following internal controls:

(i) Credit checks on customers
(ii) Training and safety leaflets for customers hiring out the equipment
(iii) Hire contracts drawn up by solicitors
(iv) Public liability insurance
(v) Maintenance contracts on the equipment

Revision activity 2

These are examples of four presentation slides and speaker notes which summarise the report's findings on the proposed capital investment for Ashbury Construction. Other approaches are possible. Learners may wish to refer to the sample slides and speaker notes when reviewing their own work.

Slide 1: The business proposition – Ashbury Construction

- An established local business with a strong track record in supporting the needs of local builders
- Suppliers of tools and building equipment
- Financially sound for over 10 years
- The company seeks £40,000 additional business finance to purchase capital equipment that can be hired out to local builders
- Plans to build new housing estates in the local area which will generate additional demand for building supplies and equipment

Slide 1 Speaker notes

- Introduce self: assistant to the owner of a local building supplies company – Ashbury Construction owned by Mr Ron Nayall.
- Strong track record in supplying tools and building materials to local builders and construction companies.
- There is a strong and loyal customer base.
- Financially sound – latest Income Statement shows a gross profit of £120,000 generating a net profit of £20,000.
- Planning permission granted for the construction of 600 low-cost housing units in the local area and this will form the basis of the business's target market.
- Local builders will be sub-contracted and will require additional supplies and capital equipment.
- Opportunities exist for the growth of Ashbury Construction within this market.

Slide 2: Financial data to support the business proposal

Financial Statement	Overview
Most recent Income Statement	Sales turnover: £200,000 Gross profit: £120,000 Net profit: £20,000
Most recent Statement of Financial Position	Assets: £88,000 Current liabilities: £15,000 Working capital: £35,000 No long-term liabilities
Projected cash flow forecast – Year 1	£1000 loan repayments per month Additional £2000 in rental income per month £203,000 annual income Year 1

Slide 2 Speaker notes

- The proposal presented in the business plan is to secure a business loan of £40,000 for the purchase of an electrical generator which will be hired out to local businesses.
- Over the five-year expected life of the Titan 100 generator there would be an estimated cash inflow of £62,000 which, when the purchase price of £40,000 is taken into account, gives a net cash inflow of £22,000.
- Gross profit margin of 60% and a net profit margin of 10% in the latest financial statements.
- Projected cash flow shows that monthly rental income would cover the additional costs of the business loan.
- Healthy statement of financial position – no long-term liabilities with a healthy working capital to meet short-term contingencies (ref: March and April in the cash flow forecast).

Slide 3: Business risks

Financial Statement	Overview	
Financial	• Planning permission refused for new housing development • Downturn in the economy • Bad debts	• Cost controls • Credit checks on customers
Legal	• Injuries caused by defective equipment • Contractual disputes	• Training and safety leaflets • Contracts drawn up by solicitors
Reputational	• Equipment breakdown	• Maintenance contracts

Slide 3 Speaker notes

- Stress that although planning permission has been rejected for the ploughfield site, planning permission has been granted for the brownfield site (600 units).
- Low-cost housing is a clear local and national priority – confident that it will go ahead.
- Current business already has in place robust risk management controls.
- Building industry is subject to strict regulations in respect of health and safety legislation.
- Ashbury Construction meets all the necessary regulatory requirements regarding health and safety.
- Business growth strategy in respect of the hiring of equipment will focus upon the existing loyal customer base who have already gone through the necessary credit checks.

Slide 4: Summary

- Established local business with strong financial base
- Application for a business loan of £40,000 to purchase an electrical generator for hire to local builders
- Positive net cash inflow generated from the equipment
- Major housing development planned
- Business risks analysed with risk management in place
- Realistic cash flow forecast showing projected increase in annual income

Slide 4 Speaker notes

- The business has grown over the last 10 years to become an established and trusted supplier of tools and equipment to local builders.
- Financial strength of the company is based upon four key factors:
  (i) high quality products
  (ii) value for money
  (iii) excellent customer service
  (iv) strong financial controls.
- These four factors have enabled the business to generate a loyal customer base – will form the basis of the proposed business proposition.
- A strong and robust business case has been made to support the proposal.
- Thank you – any questions?